MAKING
TAX
CHOICES

MAKING TAX CHOICES

Joseph J. Minarik

The Changing Domestic Priorities Series
John L. Palmer and Isabel V. Sawhill, Editors

THE URBAN INSTITUTE PRESS · WASHINGTON, D.C.

Copyright © 1985
THE URBAN INSTITUTE
2100 M Street, N.W.
Washington, D.C. 20037

Library of Congress Cataloging in Publication Data

Minarik, Joseph J., 1949–
  Making tax choices.

  (The Changing domestic priorities series)
  Includes bibliographies.
    1. Tax incidence—United States. 2. Income tax—
United States. 3. Taxation—United States. I. Title.
II. Series.
HJ2322.A3M56   1985   336.24'15'0973   85-5342
ISBN 0-87766-382-3
ISBN 0-87766-383-1 (pbk.)

Printed in the United States of America
9 8 7 6 5 4 3 2 1

THE URBAN INSTITUTE is a nonprofit policy research and educational organization established in Washington, D.C., in 1968. Its staff investigates the social and economic problems confronting the nation and government policies and programs designed to alleviate such problems. The Institute disseminates significant findings of its research through the publications program of its Press. The Institute has two goals for work in each of its research areas: to help shape thinking about societal problems and efforts to solve them, and to improve government decisions and performance by providing better information and analytic tools.

Through work that ranges from broad conceptual studies to administrative and technical assistance, Institute researchers contribute to the stock of knowledge available to public officials and to private individuals and groups concerned with formulating and implementing more efficient and effective government policy.

Conclusions or opinions expressed in Institute publications are those of the authors and do not necessarily reflect the views of other staff members, officers or trustees of the Institute, advisory groups, or any organizations which provide financial support to the Institute.

THE CHANGING DOMESTIC PRIORITIES SERIES

Listed below are the titles available, or soon to be available, in the Changing Domestic
Priorities Series

Books

THE REAGAN EXPERIMENT
   *An Examination of Economic and Social Policies under the Reagan
   Administration* (1982), John L. Palmer and Isabel V. Sawhill, editors

HOUSING ASSISTANCE FOR OLDER AMERICANS
   The Reagan Prescription (1982), James P. Zais, Raymond J. Struyk, and Thomas
   Thibodeau

MEDICAID IN THE REAGAN ERA
   Federal Policy and State Choices (1982), Randall R. Bovbjerg and John Holahan

WAGE INFLATION
   Prospects for Deceleration (1983), Wayne Vroman

OLDER AMERICANS IN THE REAGAN ERA
   Impacts of Federal Policy Changes (1983), James R. Storey

FEDERAL HOUSING POLICY AT PRESIDENT REAGAN'S MIDTERM
   (1983), Raymond J. Struyk, Neil Mayer, and John A. Tuccillo

STATE AND LOCAL FISCAL RELATIONS IN THE EARLY 1980s
   (1983), Steven D. Gold

THE DEFICIT DILEMMA
   Budget Policy in the Reagan Era (1983), Gregory B. Mills and John
   L. Palmer

HOUSING FINANCE
   A Changing System in the Reagan Era (1983), John A. Tuccillo with John L.
   Goodman, Jr.

PUBLIC OPINION DURING THE REAGAN ADMINISTRATION
   National Issues, Private Concerns (1983), John L. Goodman, Jr.

RELIEF OR REFORM?
   Reagan's Regulatory Dilemma (1984), George C. Eads and Michael Fix

THE REAGAN RECORD
   An Assessment of America's Changing Domestic Priorities (1984), John L. Palmer
   and Isabel V. Sawhill, editors (Ballinger Publishing Co.)

ECONOMIC POLICY IN THE REAGAN YEARS
   (1984), Charles F. Stone and Isabel V. Sawhill

URBAN HOUSING IN THE 1980s
   Markets and Policies (1984), Margery Austin Turner and Raymond J. Struyk

MAKING TAX CHOICES
   (1985), Joseph J. Minarik

Conference Volumes

THE SOCIAL CONTRACT REVISITED
Aims and Outcomes of President Reagan's Social Welfare Policy (1984), edited by D. Lee Bawden

NATURAL RESOURCES AND THE ENVIRONMENT
The Reagan Approach (1984), edited by Paul R. Portney

FEDERAL BUDGET POLICY IN THE 1980s (1984), edited by Gregory B. Mills and John L. Palmer

THE REAGAN REGULATORY STRATEGY
An Assessment (1984), edited by George C. Eads and Michael Fix

THE LEGACY OF REAGANOMICS
Prospects for Long-term Growth (1984), edited by Charles R. Hulten and Isabel V. Sawhill

THE REAGAN PRESIDENCY AND THE GOVERNING OF AMERICA
(1984), edited by Lester M. Salamon and Michael S. Lund

CONTENTS

FOREWORD   xv

ACKNOWLEDGMENTS   xix

ABOUT THE AUTHOR   xxi

1. MAKING A START   1
   Background: The People and the Tax System   2
   Failings of the Tax System   4
     Perceptions of Unfairness   4
     Impediments to Growth   8
     Complexity   10
   Taxation and the Budget   10
     The Deficit—Why Worry?   11
     The Deficit Outlook   16
   The Search for a Solution: Knowing Our Limits   18
     How Simple Can It Be?   18
     How Fair?   18
     How Efficient?   18
     Conflicting Goals   19
     Achieving a Balance   19

2. MAKING THE TAX SYSTEM FAIRER   21
   What Is Tax Fairness, Anyway?   21
   How Fair Is Today's Income Tax?   24
     Tax Shelters   24

Deductions and Exclusions 26
Limits and Potential 27
Fairness and the Tax Base 27
Who Pays the Income Tax? 31
Taxes and the Economy 31
Tax Burdens, 1954-1984 32
Increasing Progressivity 34
Marginal Tax Rates 36
Other Tax Preferences 38
Were All These Changes Fair? 40
Who Should Pay? 40
Which Tax Law Was Right? 43
The Income Tax and Other Taxes 44
Conclusions 47

3. MAKING THE TAX SYSTEM MORE EFFICIENT 49
What Is Tax Efficiency? 49
Resources to Run the Tax System 49
The Tax System and the Economy 50
The Slowdown in Economic Growth in the 1970s 51
Taxation and Factor Supply: The Record 52
The Supply of Labor 52
The Supply of Capital 54
Accounting for Growth 58
Conclusion 59
Experience of the 1980s—Prospects 60
Labor Supply 61
Capital Formation 61
Prospects 62
Taxation and Resource Allocation 64
Conclusions on Efficiency 65

4. MAKING THE TAX SYSTEM SIMPLER 67
What Is Tax Simplicity? 67
Simplicity for Whom? 68
Businesses 68
Individuals 69
Tax Administrators 75
Interactions 77
No-Return Taxes 80
Conclusion 82

5. MAKING THE SHORT LIST: TAXING CONSUMPTION   83
    Taxing Consumption: The Rationale   83
    Taxes on Transactions   85
       Fairness   86
       The Complication of Low-Income Relief   87
       Tax Administration   89
       Inflation   90
       International Trade   90
    Taxes on Households   91
       The Tax Deduction for Savings   91
       Economic Efficiency   92
       Administrative Advantage of the Personal Expenditure Tax   93
       Fairness   95
       The Concentration of Wealth   96
       The Personal Expenditure Tax and the Budget Deficit   97
       Tax Administration Disadvantages   99
       Taxing Corporations Under a Personal Expenditure Tax   99
       Conclusion   101
    Summary   102

6. MAKING THE SHORT LIST: TAXING INCOME   103
    The Individual Income Tax   103
       Dimensions of a Restructured Income Tax   103
       Simplification   106
       Fairness   107
       Economic Efficiency   108
       Cats and Dogs and Cats and Dogs and ...   109
       Conclusion   109
    Inflation and the Income Tax   110
    The Corporate Income Tax   114
       Why a Corporate Income Tax?   114
       Depreciation and the Investment Tax Credit   117
       Conclusion   121
    Summary   121

7. MAKING A CHOICE   123
    Economic Essentials   124
       The Tax Base   125
       Low-Income Relief   138
       Tax Rates   139
       Congressional Tax Proposals   144

The Treasury Tax Proposals   145
Restructuring and the Deficit   149
Politics—Can We Get There?   151
Taxpayers and Voters   152
Expectations and Reality   154
Business and Tax Policy   155
Conclusion   157
Implications   157
The Bottom Line   159

TABLES

1 Results of Public Opinion Polls on the Fairness of the Federal
  Income Tax, 1978 and 1979   5
2 Reconciliation of Personal and Taxable Income, 1954 and 1982   29
3 Tax Burdens on Families at Multiples of the Median Income,
  1954-1984   33
4 Marginal Tax Rates on Families at Multiples of the Median
  Income, 1954-1984   37
5 Tax Burdens on Families at Multiples of the Median Income
  With and Without Tax Preferences, 1954 and 1980   39
6 Tax Burdens on Families at Multiples of the Median Income
  Under Indexed Historical Tax Laws, 1954-1984   44
7 Tax Burdens on Families at Multiples of the Median Income
  Including Social Security Payroll Tax, Selected Years, 1954-
  1984   45
8 Average Annual Growth of Output and Labor Productivity,
  Selected Periods, 1948-1981   51
9 The Individual Income Tax Base, 1982   104
10 Effects of Alternative "Flat-Rate" Tax Systems   141
11 Amount and Sources of Income of Couples and Other Taxpayers,
  1982   153

FIGURES

1 Federal Budget Deficit as a Percentage of GNP, Fiscal Years
   1961-1989   12
2 National Debt Held by the Public as a Percentage of GNP, Fiscal
   Years 1946-1989   13
3 Federal Net Interest Payments as a Percentage of GNP, Fiscal
   Years 1946-1989   14
4 Net Credit Supplied by the Foreign Sector as a Percentage of
   GNP, 1946-1984   15
5 Adult Civilian Labor Force Participation Rate, 1947-1984   53
6 Personal and Gross Private Saving as a Percentage of GNP, 1947-
   1984   56
7 Nonresidential Investment as a Percentage of GNP, 1947-1984   58
8 Federal Individual Income Tax Liability as a Percentage of
   Personal Income, 1946-1983   143
9 Tax Burdens Under Current Law and Two Restructuring Proposals   146

FOREWORD

This book is part of The Urban Institute's Changing Domestic Priorities project, an ongoing effort to examine changes occurring in the nation's economic and social policies under the Reagan administration and analyze the effects of those changes on people, places, and institutions.

Changes in the federal income tax law were central to the incoming Reagan adminstration's 1981 policy agenda. The president proposed across-the-board reductions in personal tax rates and more rapid depreciation of business plant and equipment, which passed the Congress in slightly modified forms. The administration predicted that the new law would accelerate economic growth, increase taxpayer compliance, and reduce tax sheltering.

Whatever the new law's effect on economic growth, noncompliance has continued to increase, and public opinion of the tax system has continued to deteriorate. The 1981 actions made the tax law even more complex, with still more legal exceptions and preferences that unduly influence economic decisions, reduce federal revenues, and invite abuse. Many analysts fear that the present tax system is an inefficient instrument with which to reduce escalating federal budget deficits.

For all these reasons there has been growing sentiment for tax reform. Members of Congress have put forward alternatives to the current law, and a vigorous public debate has begun. Prospects for action accelerated in November of 1984, when the Treasury Department joined in the criticism, stating: ". . . the present U.S. income tax is complex, it is inequitable, and it interferes with the economic choices of households and businesses," and went on to propose ". . . a sweeping and comprehensive reform of the entire tax code."

In *Making Tax Choices*, Joseph J. Minarik finds that the principal public complaint, expressed in opinion polls, is that the income tax is unfair; many people believe that the affluent pay little or no tax. This perception, though exaggerated, is fed by certain realities—particularly the widely publicized growth of tax shelters and the underlying expansion of preferential provisions in the tax law. Although there is a consensus against tax sheltering, there is much less agreement on how the tax burden should be distributed among income groups. Minarik finds that the tax burden became more progressive between 1954 (the date of enactment of the current basic law) and 1980. He notes that the pattern of the burden has varied significantly from year to year, depending on economic conditions and changes in the law, and that there is thus no clear precedent for the distribution of burdens in the future.

A second complaint about the income tax is that it slows growth and distorts economic choices. As Minarik notes, currently available evidence suggests that changes in the tax law increase work, investment, and growth only modestly, if at all. He argues that the 1981 tax rate reduction has not yet yielded demonstrable benefits on any of these fronts, though much more time must pass before definitive judgments are possible. On the other hand, he finds evidence that distortions in economic choices induced by biases in the tax law reduce economic efficiency—affecting the quality if not the quantity of investment, for example.

A final complaint about the current tax system is its complexity. Minarik notes that the tax returns of most taxpayers are in fact relatively simple. The complaints arise because typical taxpayers worry that they may not be sufficiently familiar with the tax code to take advantage of the available loopholes and various special provisions in the way they believe other taxpayers do.

Given the problems with the existing law, Minarik considers some of the most frequently mentioned alternatives, including taxes on consumption. He finds that transactions-based consumption taxes, such as the value-added tax (VAT), would raise serious questions regarding fairness and would add new administrative and compliance burdens to the tax system. A personal expenditure tax collected directly from households would also raise fairness questions, would be significantly more complicated than the current income tax for most taxpayers, and would involve an extraordinarily difficult transition phase. In contrast, reform of the existing income tax would require no system-wide transition. Such reform effort could examine specific problem areas in current tax law with the objective of eliminating excessive preferences that distort economic decisions and create opportunities for abuse. With a larger tax base, Minarik shows that tax rates could be lowered to well below 40 percent and still produce $60 billion in additional revenues to alleviate the deficit problem.

Minarik notes that income tax reform would be politically difficult and—in some areas—painful. It would require repeal of many tax preferences, some long standing, to finance a corresponding reduction of tax rates. For tax reform to succeed, taxpayers must be convinced that they would gain more from the reduction of tax rates than they would lose from the repeal of existing tax preferences.

Overall, *Making Tax Choices* is a timely contribution to the debate about the necessary trade-offs and potential benefits of tax reform. This study should be an important resource for America's political leaders and taxpayers.

John L. Palmer
Isabel V. Sawhill
Editors
Changing Domestic Priorities Series

ACKNOWLEDGMENTS

The author would like to express his appreciation to Richard A. Musgrave, John L. Palmer, Joseph A. Pechman, Patricia Ruggles, Isabel V. Sawhill, Emil M. Sunley, and James M. Verdier, who read an earlier version of the manuscript and made many valuable suggestions. None of the above should be implicated in any errors. Gina Despres and Charles R. Hulten provided many helpful discussions. Mary Kate Smith helped in the preparation of the graphs, Brenda Brown, Ann Guillot, Mykki Jones, and Mary Mingo typed the manuscript, and Priscilla Taylor provided valuable editorial assistance.

The support of the Ford Foundation and John D. and Catherine T. MacArthur Foundation is also gratefully acknowledged.

Finally, the author would like to thank his wife, Eileen, and his daughters, Mara and Sara, for their patience and support during the writing of this book.

ABOUT THE AUTHOR

Joseph J. Minarik has divided his career between economic research and public service. As an academic researcher, he has investigated topics such as taxation, the distribution of income, poverty, income security policy, the consequences of inflation, and fiscal policy. His publications have appeared in the *American Economic Review*, the *Quarterly Journal of Economics*, the *National Tax Journal*, the *Review of Income and Wealth*, the Congressional Joint Economic Committee's *Special Study on Economic Change*, and volumes published by The Urban Institute and the Brookings Institution. Before joining The Urban Institute in January of 1984 as a senior research associate, Dr. Minarik served as deputy assistant director in the Tax Analysis Division of the Congressional Budget Office. He contributed to several CBO analyses of budgetary and tax issues, and advised members of both parties on proposals for tax reform.

CHAPTER 1

MAKING A START

The United States faces a double-barreled fiscal crisis. Federal budget deficits are running at all-time highs and will remain high even with consistent economic growth. At the same time, the individual income tax, which raises almost half of our revenues, is becoming increasingly unpopular and non-compliance is rising. Reducing the deficits will be doubly difficult if the tax system loses the public's trust.

For the federal tax system, however, this double crisis is also an opportunity; reducing the deficit may require—even facilitate—fundamental improvement of the tax system. Some people say that the income tax is unpopular because of how much tax we collect, not how we collect it. But just as the massive tax cuts of 1981 did not improve the public's opinion of the income tax, tax increases in the future may not cause further deterioration in the public's opinion of the tax structure itself. Although fundamental structural repair of the tax system has been discussed, actual tax legislation has always been limited in scope. Past attempts to sweeten basic restructuring with tax cuts have failed, but necessary tax increases may force a structural improvement of the tax law.

In this volume we analyze the federal corporate and individual income taxes in light of our deficit crisis. We try to pinpoint why and how the public has lost confidence in our tax system, and what can be done to regain that confidence. We compare (1) the reform of the current income tax system with alternative and additional taxes, (2) the pain of increasing taxes under the current system with the shock of higher taxes under a new system, and (3) the complexity of the current system with the confusion of change.

In the final analysis, this task is like determining the structural soundness of a building with a crumbling facade. For years our federal income tax was considered the best in the world, raising the most revenue at the least cost and earning the greatest public respect and cooperation. Our tax system may

1

still be the best in the world, but it no longer lives up to the previous standard. Is the deterioration of the income tax system, serious as it may seem, only superficial? Have we come to expect too much of the system or do we exaggerate its problems? Have our economic institutions come to rely so heavily on the tax system—including its imperfections—that no quantum change is feasible? Or have our institutions outgrown the system, leaving its foundations unable to support today's mature economy? The answers to these questions will influence tax policymaking in the years ahead.

Although the current income tax system has its weaknesses, so does its major alternative. Taxing consumption instead of income at either the household or the business level involves known problems of fairness and complexity as well as imponderable troubles of transition. The income tax, for all its flaws, is a known quantity with an invaluable institutional history both here and abroad.

Making the income tax system work better will require many hard choices. The tax law is laden with large and small rewards for particular activities and taxpayers; these subsidies cost revenue, add complexity, and invite abuse. Repeal of such provisions would be painful politically, but it would favor all taxpayers with a simpler and more certain system and lower statutory tax rates—even after extra revenues were collected to reduce the deficit. How such a tax system could be designed and whether it would be acceptable politically are the most important questions in current tax policy.

In the remainder of this chapter, we introduce the income tax, the tax policy and budget issues, and the concerns that will shape our policy choices.

Background: The People and The Tax System

The federal income tax, adopted in 1913, has long been respected everywhere. The individual income tax has grown alongside, and financed, our growing federal sector. The corporate income tax, adopted four years earlier, has been somewhat less admired, especially in the past thirty years. Nonetheless, both taxes have survived years of war, depression, and growth remarkably well.

It took a long time to add the progressive and relatively stable income taxes to a federal revenue system largely dependent on regressive and more cyclically sensitive customs duties. A Civil War income tax, though quite successful, was allowed to expire in 1872. The Congress adopted an individual income tax in 1894, but the tax was almost immediately invalidated by the Supreme Court, which ruled that because the income tax was a direct tax not apportioned among the states according to population, it violated Article I of the Constitution. The corporate income tax was enacted in 1909 as a "package deal" with the sixteenth amendment to the Constitution, which established the constitutionality of an individual income tax. The amendment was ratified in 1912, and the individual income tax was finally enacted in 1913.

The first income taxes provided only a small fraction of total federal revenues—9.7 percent in 1914.[1] Less than 1 percent of all persons, those with the highest incomes, were required to pay any income tax at all.[2] But then World War I began more than thirty years of economic ups and downs that irrevocably changed the entire tax system. Income tax rates were raised and exemptions were reduced to finance the war effort; by the end of the war, the income taxes provided 58.6 percent of total federal revenues.[3] After the war, tax rates were cut sharply; by 1929, income tax revenues had been cut by one-third from their wartime peak.[4]

The Great Depression began a long upward trend of income tax rates. Both the Hoover and Roosevelt administrations raised taxes to balance the budget, fund relief programs, and spread the burden of the hard times more fairly. Then came World War II, and tax rates were increased even further, and exemptions cut, to finance the war effort. By the end of the war, more than half of all persons in the United States paid federal income taxes;[5] the highest individual income tax rate was 94 percent,[6] and the individual and corporate taxes together supplied 80 percent of total federal revenues.[7] Respite from the high World War II tax rates was short-lived, as the Korean conflict brought back the draconian measures.

At the end of the Korean War, the tax law was recodified to remove the confusion of the many years of emergency legislation. The result was the Internal Revenue Code of 1954, which provides the basic structure of the tax law to this day. The new tax system differed in three obvious ways from the tax system of forty years earlier. First, the individual and corporate income

---

1. Sidney Ratner, *American Taxation: Its History as a Social Force in Democracy* (New York, W. W. Norton, 1942), table 1, taxes on income and profits as a percentage of total ordinary receipts.

2. Richard Goode, *The Individual Income Tax*, 2nd edition (Washington, D.C.: The Brookings Institution, 1976), table 1, p. 4.

3. Ratner, *American Taxation*, table 1, taxes on income and profits for 1919 as a percentage of total ordinary receipts.

4. Ibid.

5. Goode, *The Individual Income Tax*, table 1, p.4.

6. Joseph A. Pechman, *Federal Tax Policy*, 4th edition (Washington, D.C.; The Brookings Institution, 1983), table A-1, p. 302, rate for 1944-1945.

7. U.S. Office of Management and Budget, "Federal Government Finances: 1984 Budget Data," February 1983, processed, table 3, p. 10, data for 1944.

taxes combined provided 72.7 percent of total federal revenues,[8] compared with 9.7 percent in 1914, and so income taxes clearly had come to dominate the federal tax system. Second, individual income tax rates were much higher, at 20 percent to 91 percent, in comparison with the 1 to 7 percent range under the 1913 law,[9] and so the burden on individual taxpayers was clearly heavier. Third, about 60 percent of the household population in 1954 paid at least some tax,[10] so the tax was far more pervasive than the 1913 version which touched only 1 percent. The 1954 law remained virtually unchanged even in detail until the Kennedy-Johnson tax rate cuts of 1964.

Despite the perpetuation of high tax rates even after 1964—a range of 14 percent to 70 percent[11]—the income tax was generally recognized as the fairest tax. Polls conducted on behalf of the Advisory Commission on Intergovernmental Relations (ACIR) showed that in 1972, 36 percent of the respondents believed that the federal income tax was fairest, compared with 33 percent naming state sales taxes, the second-most-frequent response. Only 19 percent identified the federal income tax as the least fair.[12]

Since then, however, the income tax has steadily fallen in the public esteem. By 1983, another poll by ACIR showed that 35 percent of the population sampled identified the income tax as the least fair tax. In that year, 52 percent of survey respondents said that additional revenues for deficit reduction should be raised through a national sales tax, in comparison to 24 percent who would use the existing income tax.[13]

Failings of the Tax System

Perceptions of Unfairness

How did the federal income tax fall into disrepute? Responses to polls conducted by the Roper Organization on behalf of H&R Block in 1978 and 1979 identified unfairness as the major problem almost to the exclusion of the amount of tax paid, complexity, or other issues (see table 1).[14] The public

---

8. Ibid.

9. Pechman, *Federal Tax Policy*, table A-1, p. 302.

10. Goode, *The Individual Income Tax*, table 1, p. 4.

11. Pechman, *Federal Tax Policy*, table A-1, p. 302.

12. Advisory Commission on Intergovernmental Relations (ACIR), *Changing Public Attitudes on Governments and Taxes* (Washington, D.C.: U.S. Government Printing Office, 1983), appendix tables E and F-2, pp. 39 and 42.

13. Ibid., tables 2 and 3, pp. 8-9.

14. The Roper Organization, Inc., *The American Public and the Income Tax System*, vol. I: *Summary Report*, July 1978, p. 45; and *Third Annual Tax Study*, vol. I: *Summary Report*, July 1979, pp. 37 and 77.

TABLE 1

<small>RESULTS OF PUBLIC OPINION POLLS ON THE FAIRNESS OF THE FEDERAL INCOME TAX,</small>
1978 AND 1979

Question 1: **"We'd like to talk to you about the income tax system. How do you feel about the present federal income tax system—do you feel it is quite fair to most people, or reasonably fair, or somewhat unfair, or quite unfair to most people?"**

Responses	*Total Public %*[a]
Quite fair	4
Reasonably fair	28
TOTAL—*fair*	*31*
Somewhat unfair	36
Quite unfair	28
TOTAL—*unfair*	*64*
Don't know	*4*

Question 2: **"If you had to name the one thing that bothers you most about the income tax system, what would it be?"**

Responses	*Total Public %*[b]
Unfairness, inequities (net)	47
Rich people pay too little, nothing	17
Middle class, middle incomes pay too much	10
Poor pay too much	5
Big business, corporations pay too little	3
Specific additional deductions/ exemptions/credits/ needed to make system fairer	7
Shouldn't have to support those on welfare	2
Double taxation (on savings/dividends/ retirement income/etc.)	2
Should be a flat percentage rate for everyone	2
Poor pay too little	c
Unspecified inequities	11
Taxes too high	14
The way tax money is spent, wasted	10
Forms, instructions complicated/hard to file return	7
Having to pay it	3
Shouldn't owe money at end of year after having money withheld	c
Don't believe in withholding/should get interest on money withheld/should get interest on refunds	c

TABLE 1 (*continued*)

All other	2
No objections, system all right	3
Don't know/no answer	17

Question 3: **"Here is a list of some different types of people or groups. (Card shown respondent) Would you go down that list, and for each one tell me whether you think they have to pay too much in income taxes, or too little in income taxes, or about the right amount?"**

	Responses %				
	Too much	Too little	About right	Don't know	Total
Middle-income families	74	2	20	4	100
People whose income all comes from salary or wages	63	2	24	12	100
People who own their homes	50	2	33	15	100
Low-income families	47	4	37	13	100
Small business companies	38	12	30	20	100
People who live in rented homes or apartments	37	11	31	21	100
Self-employed people	29	15	28	28	100
High-income families	7	76	9	7	100
Large business corporations	5	72	10	13	100

Question 4: **There has been a lot of talk about both the need for changing the tax laws so that more people pay their fair share of taxes and the need for simplifying the tax return form people have to fill out. Of course, both of these things are important, but which one do you think should have first priority—changing the tax laws so that more people pay their fair share of taxes, or simplifying the tax return forms and instructions so that they are easier to understand and fill out, or that both are equally important?"**

	Total Public %
Changing tax laws	51
Simplifying forms and instructions	11
Equally important	32
Don't know, no answer	6
TOTAL	100

SOURCES: Questions 1 and 4—*Third Annual Tax Study*, commissioned by H&R Block Inc., and conducted by the Roper Organization Inc., July 1979, vol. I: *Summary Report*, pp. 37 and 77. Questions 2 and 3—*The American Public and the Income Tax System*, commissioned by H&R Block Inc., and conducted by the Roper Organization Inc., July 1978, vol. I: *Summary Report*, pp. 45 and 29, plus unpublished data provided by the Roper Organization.

a. Total does not equal 100 percent because of rounding.

b. Items add to more than 100 percent because multiple responses were permitted.

c. Less than 0.5 percent.

believed that average taxpayers paid too much tax, and that upper-income persons and large corporations paid too little.[15] The prevailing opinion was that more than half of the very wealthy paid no tax at all, when in fact only about 0.6 percent paid no tax.[16] This response suggests widespread misunderstanding of how the income tax operates.

This perception of unfairness—of an inappropriate balance of the tax liabilities of rich and poor—is documented in more recent polls. In 1983, ACIR asked a sample of the population to name the single most important change they would endorse to make the nation's tax system fairer. A substantial plurality, 49 percent, chose the response "to make upper-income taxpayers pay more." Only 16 percent chose the next most popular alternative—"to leave the system alone"; 13 percent chose "to cut taxes for low-income taxpayers," and 6 percent chose "to make businesses pay more, even if it reduced the number of jobs."[17] A 1984 poll commissioned by the Internal Revenue Service (IRS) found that about two-thirds of all respondents believed that they had to pay more than their fair share, and 80 percent believed that the tax system benefited the rich and was unfair to the working man or woman.[18]

When the choice of remedies was made more specific, however, taxpayers' responses took a surprising turn. In 1982, Louis Harris had found that progressive taxation won only a bare plurality of public approval. Sixty-two percent favored elimination of nearly all deductions and taxation at a flat 14 percent rate (though this majority disappeared when confronted with specific deductions to be repealed).[19] And it was to the 1983 ACIR poll just cited that a 2-to-1 majority responded that the federal government should

---

15. The Roper Organization, *The American Public*, p. 29; and idem, *Third Annual Tax Study*, p. 40.

16. The Roper Organization, *The American Public*, p. 42. In fact, in the most recent year for which tax returns had then been filed (1977), only 43 out of 7,017 tax returns with adjustable gross income of at least $500,000 (the group referred to in the survey) carried no tax liabilities—about 0.6 percent. The most recent figures available now (for 1982), using the same "over $500,000" definition of very wealthy, show 24 taxpayers paying no tax out of 29,089 returns, less than 0.1 percent. These figures both overstate and understate the nontaxable population in different respects. Some nontaxable wealthy persons earned their incomes overseas and paid more tax to their host countries than they would have to pay to the United States, and thus paid income tax, but no U.S. income tax, because of the foreign tax credit. This phenomenon is hardly abuse. Conversely, some taxpayers with considerable incomes use tax avoidance devices that reduce their measured adjusted gross income, and thus are not counted among the tax returns with at least $500,000 of income. Some of these persons may pay little or no tax.

17. ACIR, *Changing Public Attitudes*, table 7, p. 13.

18. Roscoe L. Egger, Jr., "Without Real Reform, Our Tax System Could Collapse," *Washington Post*, February 10, 1985, p.D-1.

19. "A Loss of Faith in the Progressive Tax," *Business Week*, September 6, 1982, p. 15.

increase revenues, if necessary, by imposing a new sales tax rather than by increasing the existing income tax. This juxtaposition of concern that the wealthy pay too little and average persons pay too much, on the one hand, with growing interest in a flat-rate tax or sales tax, on the other, reveals widespread mistrust and some misinformation about the fundamental workings of the income tax. If people really believe that more than half of the very wealthy pay no income tax, they will probably conclude that a low flat-rate income tax with no tax avoidance opportunities, or even a national sales tax, would increase the share of the tax burden borne by the wealthy. Because more sophisticated analysis suggests that the effect would be the opposite, these poll responses disturbingly suggest that the public might not know how to get what it wants.

Another indication of popular disapproval of the income tax is growing noncompliance with the tax law. The IRS has estimated that the revenue lost through noncompliance, with respect only to income of individuals obtained legally, increased from $25 billion in 1973 (23 percent of the amount actually collected) to $75 billion in 1981 (27 percent of actual collections).[20] Thus, noncompliance grew at an annual rate of 14.6 percent, faster than actual collections. The IRS found a trend toward increasing understatement of most types of income and increasing overstatement of exemptions and deductions for allowable business expenses. There need not be any esoteric cause— surely the tax evaders would rather keep their money than give it to the federal government or anyone else—but public dissatisfaction with the income tax could be a factor.[21]

Impediments to Growth

Economists have long acknowledged that taxation may slow the economy by reducing work effort, saving, and investment, and by distorting the al-

---

20. Department of the Treasury, Internal Revenue Service, *Income Tax Compliance Research: Estimates for 1973-1981* (Washington, D.C.: U.S. Government Printing Office, July 1983), table I-1, p. 3. These estimates have their critics. The most controversial part of the IRS methodology is the estimation of amounts of unreported income based on the success rate of IRS audits in reporting such income (see *Income Tax Compliance Research*, appendix B, pp. 49-70). The questions about this methodology challenge only the estimated *size* of the tax gap, however; the faster *rate of growth* of the tax gap compared to tax collections is confirmed by actual IRS audit experience (see *Income Tax Compliance Research*, table B-2, p. 60).

21. Ann D. Witte and Diane F. Woodbury, "What We Know About Factors Affecting Compliance with Tax Laws," in *Invitational Conference on Income Tax Compliance*, sponsored by the Section of Taxation of the American Bar Association, March 16-19, 1983, pp. 199-228; M. W. Spicer and S. B. Lanstedt, "Understanding Tax Evasion," *Public Finance*, vol. 31, no. 2, 1976, pp. 295-305; Michael W. Spicer and Lee A. Becker, "Fiscal Inequity and Tax Evasion: An Experimental Approach," *National Tax Journal*, vol. 33, no. 2, 1980, pp. 171-75; Roscoe L. Egger, Jr., "Without Real Reform, Our Tax System Could Collapse."

location of scarce resources. Any tax will reduce incentives and distort resource allocation to some degree, but until recently the effects of the U.S. tax system were believed to be small.

Some economists have argued that our income tax system slows growth substantially, because high tax rates reduce the incentive to work and save.[22] Phased-in across-the-board reductions in the tax rates to a range of from 11 to 50 percent were justified in 1981 on the basis of this so-called supply-side economics theory. As a result of these tax cuts, statutory rates have become substantially lower than in the late 1960s, when growth was extremely rapid, and are even more markedly reduced from the 1954-1964 period, which also saw considerable economic growth. Yet supply-side arguments for still lower tax rates persist.[23]

The current tax law is also alleged to slow growth by distorting the allocation of resources. The law now contains more than 100 preferential provisions that reduce or eliminate tax for people who earn or spend their incomes in particular ways.[24] (These provisions are called "tax expenditures," because a tax preference is like a spending program that pursues the same purpose.) These special tax provisions have accumulated over time with little legislative oversight or review. All these provisions are well intended; some are designed to cushion hardship, others to induce worthwhile forms of activity such as saving, homeownership, or energy conservation. Nonetheless, some are used by shrewd investors in unforeseen combinations that reduce tax liabilities but produce no other benefit to the taxpayer or society. All preferences move resources from the more efficient uses to which they would be put without such interference in the market process. Furthermore, by reducing tax revenue, such provisions force the federal government to charge higher tax rates on all other forms of income, thereby discouraging work, saving, and investment.

---

22. Prominent examples include Martin Feldstein, "The Welfare Cost of Capital Income Taxation," *Journal of Political Economy*, vol. 86 (April 1978, pt. 2), pp. 29-51; and Jerry A. Hausman, "Labor Supply," in Henry J. Aaron and Joseph A. Pechman, eds., *How Taxes Affect Economic Behavior* (Washington, D.C.: The Brookings Institution, 1981), pp. 27-71. Barry P. Bosworth, *Tax Incentives and Economic Growth* (Washington, D.C.: The Brookings Institution, 1984) provides a survey and critique.

23. Chapter 2 shows that taxpayers have climbed up through the tax rate brackets somewhat faster than the tax rates in any given bracket have been cut, however.

24. Congressional Budget Office, *Tax Expenditures: Current Issues and Five-Year Budget Projections for Fiscal Years 1984-1988* (Washington, D.C.: U.S. Government Printing Office, October 1983).

Complexity

A tax system can also consume excess resources through unnecessary complexity, and complexity is a complaint frequently made against our tax system. Complexity has been introduced through the multitude of tax expenditures just mentioned. When particular types of income or expenditure are favored, every taxpayer naturally wants to take advantage; and so other types of income or expenditure are redefined to fit the legal requirements. The government retaliates with regulations, taxpayers respond with litigation, and case law is piled on top of the code itself. The more generous the tax preference, the more ardent the taxpayers seeking to take advantage, and the more complex tax administration necessarily becomes.

Even so, tax complexity does not come only from tax preferences. A complex economy will necessarily breed some complexity in the tax system. Just defining income can be complex. Some tax preferences are justified in part because it is simpler to exempt certain types of income than to define and measure them.

The pursuit of fairness also can lead to complexity. Some tax preferences are intended to provide relief from extraordinary expenses. However noble this purpose, defining those extraordinary expenses and limiting the relief to them can be complex.

Taxation and the Budget

Our tax system is straining under these perceptions of unfairness and economic distortions, but worse still, it may not raise enough revenue. The federal budget deficit is extremely large by historical standards, and without changes in policy the deficit is projected to grow still larger, even with consistent economic growth. These large deficits could be costly over the long run, at best, or explosively dangerous, at worst.

In theory, the questions of how much revenue to raise (the deficit issue) and how to raise it (the structural tax reform issue) can be largely separated, but in practice, the two questions are linked. Some analysts fear that an increasingly unpopular income tax system, with falling compliance and possibly serious distortionary effects, cannot be a vehicle for deficit reduction. Analysts also are uncertain whether the Congress and the public would accept the pain and dislocation of structural tax change without the motivation of the need to reduce the deficit. For these reasons, it is important to see the tax policy issues in a budgetary context.

The Deficit—Why Worry?

The budget deficit issue is highly controversial and often misunderstood. The projected federal budget deficits are troubling because of their size and their timing. Budget deficits are certainly not immoral, and in some circumstances they are inevitable and helpful. For example, if the economy is weak and unemployment is high or rising, a deficit can put money into the hands of families and businesses, stimulate spending in the private sector, and put idle resources back to work. Attempting to reduce such a deficit with higher taxes or lower spending would be self-defeating and would slow economic recovery.

In the recent recession and its early recovery, the large federal deficits and consequent borrowing needs were not troublesome because the recession was so deep. Consumers cut back on their spending, and so their credit demands were modest. Businesses did not need to expand, and therefore to borrow, because they had significant idle capacity. Then the first surge of needed business investment was financed largely by the bounceback of profits that typically comes early in a recovery, again keeping business borrowers out of the credit markets.

As the recovery and expansion proceed, however, business and consumer borrowing will grow. Under current federal budget policy, a collision with federal demands for credit is unavoidable. The Reagan administration projects the fiscal 1985* deficit at more than $200 billion, about 5 percent of GNP, which is unprecedentedly high for the third year of an economic recovery and expansion. The projections of the Congressional Budget Office (CBO) are similar (see figure 1). Even if the economy were now at full employment (reasonably defined), a "structural deficit" (so called because it would be caused by conscious budget decisions, not by a temporary recession) would remain. The CBO projects that the federal deficit for fiscal 1989 will be $263 billion (equal to 4.9 percent of projected GNP) and that the structural deficit in 1989 will be even larger than that of fiscal 1985.[25] Such a condition in a period of continuing expansion also is without precedent.

The current and projected deficits have crossed a line into a new category that might be termed "mega-deficits." Since World War II, even though the federal government has run deficits consistently, those deficits were small

---

*References to years in this volume are to calendar years unless otherwise indicated. Fiscal years are used only for federal government budget statistics, which are generally computed for the federal fiscal year (October 1 through September 30).

25. Congressional Budget Office, *The Economic and Budget Outlook: An Update* (Washington, D.C.: U.S. Government Printing Office, 1984), table III-1, p. 55.

FIGURE 1

FEDERAL BUDGET DEFICIT AS A PERCENTAGE OF GNP,
FISCAL YEARS 1961–1989

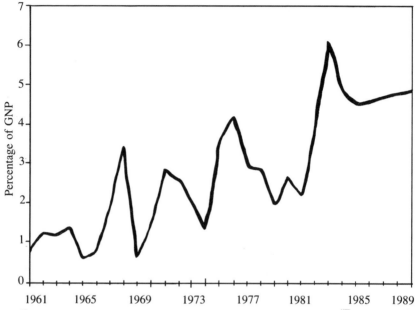

SOURCES: Office of Management and Budget, "Federal Government Finances: 1984 Budget
Data," February 1983, tables 1 and 13; Congressional Budget Office, *The Economic
and Budget Outlook: An Update*, August 1984, table III-1, p. 55.

enough that the economy grew faster than the accumulating national debt.
(Inflation helped here, depreciating the real value of the outstanding debt.)
Thus, when measured next to our income and wealth, the national debt was
shrinking. But the recent and projected deficits are so large that they are
building up our national debt at a rate faster than the economy is growing,
reversing the trend of almost forty years (see figure 2). Already the deficits
of the past five years have eroded twenty years of progress in outgrowing the
national debt. The interest cost of servicing that debt also is growing faster
than GNP and, in fact, faster than federal revenues or other federal spending
(see figure 3). If such deficits were to continue unchecked into the indefinite
future, the debt service burden eventually would equal all production in the
economy. At that point, the government would have to impose 100 percent
tax rates, confiscating all incomes, just to service the national debt.

FIGURE 2

NATIONAL DEBT HELD BY THE PUBLIC AS A PERCENTAGE OF GNP,
FISCAL YEARS 1946–1989

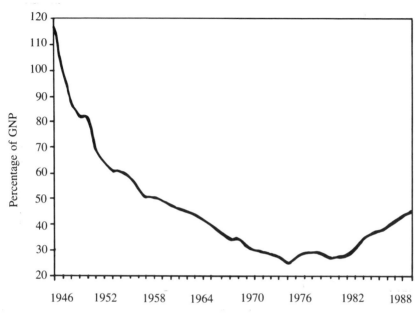

SOURCES: Office of Management and Budget, "Federal Government Finances: 1984 Budget
Data," February 1983, table 15, pp. 101–102; Congressional Budget Office, unpublished data.

Includes debt held by the Federal Reserve System.

Even short of this extreme predicament, however, large deficits and the
consequent growing national debt impose significant costs. The larger the
debt, the more taxes the federal government must collect just to meet its
annual debt service burden. Because those taxes impose distortions and costs
on the economy, as well as pain on the taxpayers, we should hold the debt
down. The longer we wait to take action on the deficits, the larger the
accumulated national debt and hence the larger the debt service burden.

A further cost of deficits is that they can reduce our long-term capital
formation. At any given time there is in the economy a certain supply of
loanable funds—savings of individuals, businesses, financial intermediaries,
and governments. There is also a certain demand for those funds—from
persons who want to buy homes or other consumer durables, from businesses
that want to invest in plant and equipment, and from borrowing governments.
All else being equal, if the federal government needs to borrow more, it must

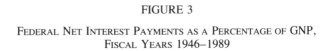

FIGURE 3

FEDERAL NET INTEREST PAYMENTS AS A PERCENTAGE OF GNP,
FISCAL YEARS 1946–1989

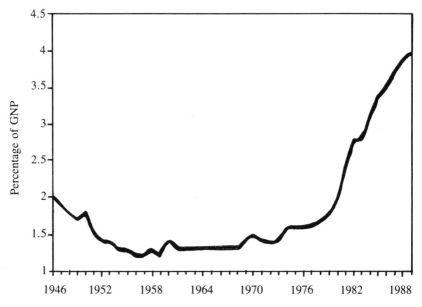

SOURCES: Office of Management and Budget, "Federal Government Finances: 1984 Budget
           Data," February 1983, table 13, pp. 86–90; Congressional Budget Office, *The
           Economic and Budget Outlook: An Update*, August 1984, table III-5, p. 62.

bid those funds away from other borrowers, raising interest rates and reducing
investment, home building, and other credit-sensitive activities—thereby reducing our future standard of living. Between 1984 and 1988, the federal
government could absorb as much as half of the likely net domestic savings.[26]
By all historical standards, the remainder of our national savings will not be
enough to accommodate the credit demands that would be expected of businesses and consumers at that stage of an economic expansion.

   The effects of the deficits could be less than catastrophic. From the
recession through 1984, we have met our credit needs in large part by borrowing from foreigners (see figure 4), moderating the depressing effect on
investment. This borrowing could continue for a time. But further and ex-

_____

   26. Isabel V. Sawhill and Charles F. Stone, *Economic Policy in the Reagan Years* (Washington, D.C.: The Urban Institute Press, 1984), table 11.

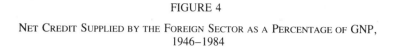

FIGURE 4

NET CREDIT SUPPLIED BY THE FOREIGN SECTOR AS A PERCENTAGE OF GNP,
1946–1984

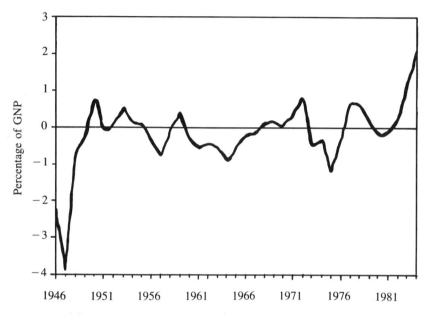

SOURCE: Board of Governors of the Federal Reserve System, "Flow of Funds Accounts,"
various numbers.

panded reliance on foreign capital will require continued high interest rates
to attract that capital and a continued high exchange value of the dollar. To
lend here (that is, to buy a debt security of a U.S. firm or government),
foreigners must first buy dollars; the resultant increased demand for the dollar
increases its exchange value with other currencies. Imports become less expensive here and our exports become more expensive abroad, so American
firms selling tradable goods become less competitive. Furthermore, foreign
investors will reap the return to an increasing share of the capital in the United
States. If all goes well there will be no bang, but the U.S. economy could
whimper indefinitely.

The more extreme risks of the deficits are far worse. Large and continuing
deficits, which are stimulative, place a very heavy load on monetary policy
to hold the economy in balance and inflation in check. Because federal deficits
are well outside historical bounds, because real (inflation-adjusted) interest

rates are at historically high levels, because the economy is approaching full employment, because our trade balance is becoming increasingly unfavorable, and because many debtor nations around the world are straining to meet their interest obligations to U.S. banks, the margin for error in monetary policy appears to be significantly reduced. And in the face of all of these imponderables, the consequences of any miscalculation or unexpected economic shock could well be great.

The Deficit Outlook

Even with current economic policy, there is some chance that the large projected deficits will not materialize. The CBO projections are based on an historically average economic expansion, with real economic growth of about 4 percent over its duration. Obviously, there are precedents for exceeding the historical average rate of growth. But these projections are optimistic in assuming that consistent (if moderate) growth proceeds all the way through 1989 without interruption. Considering our high real interest rates, trade deficits, and shaky loans to other nations, it would be good fortune indeed if our economy could grow consistently with no significant pause or recession.

Even more rapid economic growth would not help very much. Economic growth of about 5 percent per year (one percentage point faster) would leave the deficit at 3 percent of GNP, still outside the historical range for an economy so close to full employment.[27] And this more optimistic forecast requires the same continued smooth sailing as the baseline projection, but with the economy growing faster and the risks consequently greater.

The downside of reliance on good fortune—that is, inaction—is the long-term effect on the national debt if fortune is bad. A recession would decrease tax revenues, increase transfer payments, and send the deficit well above the current forecast. Such an increment to the national debt would raise debt service obligations still further. Cutting the deficit to hold down the debt during a recession would be extremely painful. And with so many economic variables already outside their historical ranges, the policy choices in a recession and the economy's responses to them would be most unclear.

In light of these risks, most experts agree that we must take action, and that spending cuts, though essential, cannot be enough to close the large and growing deficit gap. Thus, tax increases will be required as well.

---

27. *The Economic and Budget Outlook: An Update*, pp. 70-71. This assumes that growth in output is driven by greater demand, meaning that unemployment and federal government transfer payments fall. If output grew through productivity increases, leaving unemployment and transfer payments relatively higher, deficit reduction would be even less.

Determining the appropriate amount of deficit reduction, the timing, and the division between outlay reductions and revenue increases is beyond the scope of this book;[28] but a sense of orders of magnitude is needed to choose the best deficit remedy. The highest acceptable deficit near full employment is probably about 2 percent of GNP, which is higher than the deficit of any near-full employment year since World War II apart from the time of the Vietnam War buildup. For fiscal 1989, when the economy will approach full employment if moderate growth continues, this calculation implies a deficit of no more than about $110 billion, or roughly $150 billion less than the deficit projected under current policy.

Not all of a $150 billion deficit reduction need be provided through tax increases; presumably, some portion would come from reductions in outlays. And any deficit reduction in the intervening years would reduce net interest obligations in 1989, and thus obviate the need for at least some policy action in that year. Assuming a fifty-fifty split of outlay reductions and tax increases, and further assuming some earlier reduction of the deficit, the necessary tax increase in 1989 would be a minimum of about $60 billion.

To put this figure in context, tax revenues from the individual income tax under current policy are projected at $500 billion in fiscal 1989, projected corporate revenues are $100 billion, and total revenues from all taxes are just over $1 trillion. Thus, the necessary tax increase would be equivalent to about a 6 percent increase in all taxes, or about 10 percent in the individual and corporate income taxes alone. Obviously, such an increase would represent a substantial takeback of the 23 percent tax rate cuts that were phased in from 1981 through 1984.

Increasing taxes by such magnitudes must be painful, but a flawed basic tax structure only makes matters worse. Taxpayers who believe they are overtaxed in comparison with other taxpayers will resent simple increases in the tax rates. Tax rate increases do not reach people who now successfully avoid tax. (As Senate Finance Committee Chairman Robert Dole is reported to have said in dismissing a 10 percent surtax proposal in 1982, "Ten percent of nothing is nothing.") An increase in the tax rate would only aggravate any noncompliance caused by perceptions of unfairness and any distortions caused by unequal taxation of different investments. So for the long haul, tax restructuring could be a prerequisite for deficit reduction.

---

28. This topic is discussed in John L. Palmer and Gregory Mills, *The Deficit Dilemma* (Washington, D.C.: The Urban Institute Press, 1983).

The Search for a Solution: Knowing Our Limits

The many flaws in the tax system prove that there is room for improvement, but this is a proof by default. The sad fact is that there is no single, easy solution to our many tax problems.

How Simple Can It Be?

Recent tax-restructuring proposals have emphasized simplicity, and taxpayers surely would appreciate the shortest possible forms and the simplest possible computations. Nonetheless, there are practical limits. However simple the tax structure, businesses need accounting to determine their profits. Some of the most complex individual income tax questions are the determination of dependent and head of household status, and those questions would remain under most tax structures. Certain bedrock itemized deductions, too, such as those for mortgage interest and charitable contributions, will probably remain.

How Fair?

Even fairness, in the sense of appropriate treatment of each individual taxpayer relative to all others, is necessarily limited. Our traditional standard of fairness is equality of taxes for taxpayers with equal ability to pay. Obviously, however, ability to pay is a subjective concept. In seeking a practical measure of ability to pay, the current tax law allows deductions for certain extraordinary expenses (high medical expenses or casualty losses, for example). Some people might argue that these deductions do not go far enough; the law makes no allowance for people who live in regions where rents are high or face higher costs of everyday living because of disability, for instance. The range of taxpayer circumstances is just about infinite, and no practical tax law could account for every gradation of well-being.

In addition, people with more income tend to pay more tax, but below a certain point people with less income do not pay less tax; once the income tax goes to zero, further gradation stops. (There is an exception only for households with children, through the refundable earned-income tax credit, but this is a small and by all accounts underutilized provision.) Despite considerable academic interest, we have not yet found a workable negative income tax; some people might call this another limit on tax fairness.

How Efficient?

As was noted earlier, any feasible tax will reduce economic efficiency in some way. A tax on income from work or on consumption discourages working to earn money to spend. Taxes on investment income discourage saving and, given the difficulty of measuring investment income, might distort the allocation of investment as well. Any tax also uses up some resources for compliance and administration. From the point of view of economic efficiency, therefore, any tax is an evil, however necessary.

Conflicting Goals

Finally, every goal of the tax system is in some sense in conflict with the others. Clearly, we could have tax deductions to compensate for every difference in taxpayers' abilities to pay, from the rent they pay down to the most trivial expenses, but such a tax system would be hopelessly complex. We must balance compensation for special circumstances against the complexity that such allowances will cause. Similarly, incentives for chosen kinds of investments necessarily discriminate against others and will cause complexity. And an income tax can achieve stark simplicity only by omitting provisions to alleviate hardship and encourage investment, charitable giving, homeownership, or other desirable activities.

Achieving a Balance

So in virtually every respect, tax policymaking is a search for a balance. There is an obvious need for more revenue, but higher tax rates would burden taxpayers, increase economic distortions, and decrease incentives. The tax system needs restructuring, but quantum changes could cause confusion, disrupt existing contractual commitments, and impose gains and losses on different groups. And although a simpler, fairer, and more efficient tax system would be welcome, no one of these objectives can be pursued to the exclusion of the others. If we forget the cost in simplicity of pursuing greater fairness or efficiency, or vice versa, we could wind up with a system that is worse, all things considered, than what we have now.

To improve the tax system, we must understand these constraints. In the remainder of this volume, we analyze each objective of the tax system and how objectives conflict with one another. We evaluate our budgetary needs in the context of our tax system, we weigh our tax policy options against our tax objectives and our deficit.

Raising taxes is never painless. But if taxes must go up, we should look for the least painful way, for the taxpayers and for the economy. A close examination will suggest that the short-term pain in a restructuring of the income tax can yield a much greater long-term benefit.

CHAPTER 2

MAKING THE TAX SYSTEM
FAIRER

Proponents of tax reforms tend to claim fairness in absolute terms. The Bible and tithing are cited to justify 10 percent flat-rate taxes. Taxes "with no deductions or exclusions" are proposed. An end to noncompliance and a flow of additional tax revenues from the underground economy are counted as likely benefits.

Unfortunately, fairness in a tax system cannot even be defined, much less measured scientifically. Measures of the "true" incomes of different taxpayers are inevitably subjective.[1] And even assuming that we had a correct definition of income, the "fair" amount of tax for any given taxpayer would be even more controversial.

With the fairness of any tax system a matter of opinion, judgment must play an important role in tax restructuring.

What Is Tax Fairness, Anyway?

To decide whether a tax system is fair, we first must decide what tax fairness is. There is no simple and obvious definition. Given many different taxpayers in different circumstances, we cannot determine instantly the fairness of our current income tax or of any conceivable alternative.

To analyze tax fairness, economists have split the issue into two parts: *horizontal equity* and *vertical equity*. A tax system is horizontally equitable if identically situated people pay the same tax; a tax system is vertically equitable if it treats differently situated people in appropriately different ways.

Each of these standards of fairness obviously is somewhat ambiguous. Horizontal equity is hard to interpret because no two taxpayers are exactly

---

1. Some experts now challenge income as an appropriate basis for taxation, preferring consumption. Taxes on consumption are discussed in chapter 5.

alike in terms of both income and household expenses. The range of individual circumstances that we might take into account to determine if taxpayers are equally well off is enormous. Different taxpayers incur different expenses in the course of earning their incomes (commuting, work clothes, costs of investment research, and so on). Some of these are true costs of earning income and thus should be tax deductible in arriving at *net* income; but others are more like personal consumption. Similarly, all households incur some extraordinary and unrewarding expenses, like medical care costs and casualty losses, that properly might be deductible in measuring their ability to pay; but even those expenses are sometimes hard to separate from ordinary consumption (witness horror stories about medically prescribed indoor swimming pools and comestic surgery).[2] So with no really identical taxpayers, the whole concept is somewhat subjective.

Even more ambiguous is the concept of vertical equity. Given that one taxpayer is better off than another, how much more tax should the better-off pay? Theorists have wrestled with this question without finding a definitive answer.[3] At least one extreme has been demarcated, however; there has been no convincing case that an income tax should increase less than in proportion to income. (Arguments that a regressive tax—one that declines as a proportion of income—would encourage work and investment by high-income persons generally are rejected on humanitarian or fairness grounds.) The "pure flat-rate tax," a fixed proportion of income with no exemptions or deductions of any kind, is therefore an outer bound. But even most flat-tax advocates would allow some exemption to free taxpayers with low incomes from paying tax; and so historically there has been broad consensus for a progressive income tax, that is, one that increases in percentage terms as income increases.

But how progressive should the income tax be? Even a flat-rate tax can be made more progressive with a larger exemption and a higher tax rate, and so merely arguing for a flat tax does not answer the question. But ever since its enactment in 1913, our income tax has used graduated rates to achieve more progressivity than could be had with a flat rate.[4] Now the graduated

---

2. "Taking the Plunge: How One Taxpayer Justified a Swimming Pool Deduction," *Wall Street Journal*, August 31, 1983, p. 1; "No on Tattoos," *New York Times*, August 3, 1982, p. A-14.

3. An early contribution to this issue is the equal sacrifice theory as expressed by A. C. Pigou, *A Study in Public Finance*, 3rd edition, (London: Macmillan and Co., 1951). Walter J. Blum and Harry Kalven, Jr., *The Uneasy Case for Progressive Taxation* (Chicago: University of Chicago Press, 1953) analyze these arguments and present their case for a flat-rate tax. More recent discussions by Blum, W. Allen Wallis, and James Tobin are included in Colin D. Campbell, ed., *Income Redistribution* (Washington, D.C.: American Enterprise Institute, 1977), part 3.

4. In practice, personal exemptions and standard deductions supply the greatest progressivity at lower income levels; rate graduation has the greatest effect further up the income scale.

rates seem to be under some popular attack—a surprising development, given the support in opinion polls (noted in the preceding chapter) for heavier taxation of the better-off.

Although it is apparent that people want some progressivity, it is equally apparent that they want progressivity only within limits. In 1980 and 1981, a majority of the electorate voted for and supported Ronald Reagan and his 23 percent across-the-board tax cuts; this support was reaffirmed in 1984. Those tax cuts helped the well-to-do the most in dollar terms. And in hindsight, people also approve of the Kennedy-Johnson tax cuts of 1964, which sharply reduced the maximum rates and taxes of the well-off (although low-income taxpayers benefited even more in percentage terms from an increased standard deduction).[5] So recent history suggests that people do not want anything like confiscatory taxation, even for the taxpayers with the highest incomes; but there is no consensus on just how progressive the income tax should be.

Because fairness is a complex concept about which there will always be disagreement, the public's preferences at any given time will remain unclear. Opinion polls can help, but the context and wording of polling questions can be very important, and interpretation can be difficult. The uncertainty of the subject matter and of public opinion compounds the task of the policymaker and policy analyst.

Given the limits of our knowledge and the diversity of public opinion, there is no single fair tax system in any objective, scientific sense. Any proposed tax could be more or less fair than any other from any individual taxpayer's point of view. A fair tax system can only be found through an inevitably controversial decision of the democratic process and the people's elected representatives. In other words, fairness is what the people say it is.

Another element of tax fairness becomes pertinent when we contemplate change. Not only the level of taxes, but also any change in taxes, might be a criterion of fairness. People make long-term financial commitments, including the purchase of homes and cars, and they expect some regularity in their financial affairs so that they can meet those commitments. If taxes are increased substantially and without warning, some taxpayers' budgets will be unable to absorb the shock. This danger is particularly important when asset values as well as tax liabilities are affected. To take an extreme example, if repeal of the mortgage interest deduction were to increase certain homeowners' taxes beyond their ability to pay, they could not just turn around and sell their houses; the houses' value on the market would be reduced by the interest

---

5. Congressional Quarterly, *Congress and the Nation 1945-1964: A Review of Government and Politics in the Postwar Years* (Washington, D.C.: Congressional Quarterly Inc., 1965), p. 438.

deduction repeal that any prospective purchasers would surely take into account. The taxpayers might have no way out.

Therefore, because there is no certainty about standards of tax fairness, and because fairness is a necessary criterion in any change, we must move with caution.

How Fair Is Today's Income Tax?

The American people give our income tax low marks for fairness, as the opinion polls cited in chapter 1 show, so if fairness is what the people say it is, the income tax doesn't have it. Both the level of negative polling responses and the increase in such responses are disturbing. So is the evidence of decreasing compliance with the income tax.

Tax Shelters

One recent phenomenon may both cause and confirm such polling responses: the rise of the tax shelter. Tax shelters are investments that use a combination of tax law provisions (the investment tax credit, accelerated depreciation, the deductibility of interest expense, and sometimes others) plus a bit of creative accounting to create large, temporary, artificial accounting losses.[6] These losses can be used to offset or "shelter" large incomes from other sources, leaving low measured incomes for tax purposes, and therefore low tax liabilities. At some point, the flow of tax losses runs dry, and the taxpayer recovers the initial investment (often as capital gains income at a reduced tax rate). The taxpayer may then turn around and buy another tax shelter to offset that income, and so the cycle continues.

Tax shelters are typically organized as limited partnerships, which allow the tax losses to "pass through" to the partners on a year-by-year basis. (The losses of a corporation, in contrast, are not deductible by the shareowners.) Tax shelter investments can be (1) in sailboats that are ostensibly used for business but are really bought for enjoyment and for tax reduction purposes; (2) in farm animals that are rapidly depreciated; or (3) in books, master audio recordings, billboards, or many other forms of property. Historically, however, two of the most popular forms of tax shelters have been investments in real estate (using the deductibility of interest, the accelerated tax depreciation of buildings, and their sale for capital gains income after much of the depre-

---

6. Much more commonplace investments such as owner-occupied homes and Individual Retirement Accounts are sometimes called "tax shelters" but they are not included in this discussion.

ciation has been deducted) and oil and gas properties (using the special tax preferences of "expensing," that is, immediate deduction of intangible drilling costs, and percentage depletion).[7]

The power of these tax-motivated investments can be considerable. In its 1984 listing of the 400 wealthiest persons in the United States, *Forbes* reported that 71 derived their fortunes principally from real estate and 74 from oil and gas.[8] It might be surprising that one in six of these largest fortunes was accumulated in a real estate industry that, in the aggregation of all of its partnership investments, recorded a net loss of over $11 billion in 1982. In the same year, oil and gas extraction partnerships, the source of another one-sixth of the nation's largest fortunes, reported a total net loss of almost $8 billion.[9]

Tax sheltering is booming, particularly since the 1981 tax cuts, which included a generous liberalization of tax depreciation provisions. In fact, in 1981, the entire partnership sector of the economy reported an overall net loss for the first time in the twenty-five-year history of the compilation of separate partnership statistics.[10] Tax shelters were assigned an important role in this development.[11] In 1982 (the latest year for which data are available), the overall net loss was even greater, and tax shelter activity was indicated as the main reason for the loss.[12] Even the 1982 reduction in the highest marginal individual income tax rate to 50 percent, which was predicted to make the shelters much less attractive, did not reverse this growth. At the same time, there has been more advertising and editorial coverage of tax shelters, so typical taxpayers have been exposed to both legal tax avoidance and marginally legal manipulation.

The liberalization of tax depreciation is not the only change in the tax system that facilitates tax sheltering. Also in 1981, the investment tax credit was increased for some investments. In 1978, the exclusion for long-term capital gains was increased. Additional targeted tax incentives for particular activities have opened new tax shelter opportunities in such an unlikely area

---

7. These tax preferences for oil and gas are discussed in chapter 7.

8. "Forbes Four Hundred," *Forbes*, vol. 134, October 1, 1984, pp. 76-165.

9. Patrick Piet, "Partnership Returns, 1982," *Statistics of Income Bulletin*, vol. 4, Summer 1984, pp. 85-95.

10. This is not to suggest that all partnerships are tax shelters, or even that all partnerships that lose money are tax shelters. It merely indicates that the losses of the partnerships that are tax shelters exceed the net incomes of the partnerships that are not.

11. Patrick Piet, "Partnership Returns for 1981 Reflect Tax Shelter Activity," *Statistics of Income Bulletin*, vol. 3, Winter 1983-84, pp. 29-40.

12. Piet, "Partnership Returns, 1982," p. 85.

as research and development. All these provisions have worthwhile purposes, but when combined they make tax shelters possible.

With tax sheltering becoming easier and more profitable, it is hardly surprising that use of shelters should increase, nor is it surprising that the bulk of the taxpayers who cannot profit from tax shelters resent those who can. The rationale of the progressive income tax always has been that people who earned more income paid more tax; it is disturbing to taxpayers at the bottom and the middle of the economic ladder to learn that this isn't always true.

What is particularly offensive about tax shelters is that they reward purely tax-motivated behavior. Most tax shelters provide no useful service to society or the economy—they involve only the exchange of ownership of assets that already exist, or the building of new assets that yield no profit other than tax reduction—and they allow some people to apply special skills to the tax system for their own profit. So the tax law itself is used for personal enrichment, rather than for providing revenue for public purposes as it was intended. Public opinion is further offended because only top-bracket taxpayers can play; shelter-generated deductions are not worth their cost if the taxpayer's marginal tax rate is not high. Widely publicized instances of tax sheltering are probably an important cause of opinion poll complaints that wealthy people pay too little tax.

Deductions and Exclusions

Many tax deductions or exclusions favor some people over others. Particular industries—oil, timber, and banking, among others—have tax law provisions that reduce their tax liabilities. Some personal tax deductions, such as tax deductions for homeowners, favor particular groups.

Tax deductions and exclusions in general can offend many tax analysts' perceptions of fairness. If high-income taxpayers are permitted to deduct a dollar of medical expenses or exclude a dollar's worth of employer-paid medical insurance, as two examples, their taxes are reduced by as much as fifty cents. In contrast, the same deduction or exclusion is worth as little as eleven cents to low-paid workers. In fact, no preference is worth anything at all if the taxpayers do not have enough income to owe tax; and itemized deductions are worthless if taxpayers claim the standard deduction (or zero-bracket amount). If these tax preferences are intended to help people to afford medical care, then obviously more of the benefit is directed to the people who need help least. This phenomenon of the largest benefit of tax deductions and exclusions going to those with the highest incomes is referred to as an "upside-down subsidy." (This criticism does not apply to deductions of costs of earning income, which are needed to arrive at properly taxable net income.)

The upside-down subsidies (and the zero benefit for people who are nontaxable or who claim the standard deduction) obviously limit the potential fairness of the tax system. In an ideal world, some cosmic computer might evaluate every taxpayer's income and expenses, deducting all unrewarding expenses (including some medical costs, for example) to arrive at a true measure of well-being. In our imperfect world, however, we must impose restrictions and rules of thumb to keep the system capable of being administered and understood. A standard deduction is an administrative necessity, easing the recordkeeping burden of most taxpayers and the clerical load on the IRS. And a tax system that extended subsidies to the entire population, including those who paid no tax, would be far more intrusive and complex than the current law.

Limits and Potential

So it is clear that our tax system cannot be fair in an absolute sense. The gaps in our knowledge, the diversity of public opinion, and the need for simplicity dictate that we achieve fairness mostly through rough-justice approximations, and only within limits.

But it is equally clear that our current tax law does not test those limits. It contains myriad exceptions to its general rules which unfairly favor some taxpayers. The extreme use of tax preferences to reduce tax without true economic benefit—tax sheltering—is probably the greatest violation of the public's sense of tax fairness.

Fairness and the Tax Base

If the public is convinced that the income tax is unfair, we need to know why. Has there been any measurable deterioration in the performance of the tax system?

Because fairness is an amorphous concept, there is no simple quantitative measure. Nonetheless, one principle of fairness in taxation is that, in the absence of some strong justification, all income should be subject to tax; exclusions and deductions should be held to minimum. Leakages from the theoretically attainable individual income tax base can be measured, and their trend over time can indicate the prevalence of potentially unfair exceptions in the tax law.

The standard measure of the potential tax base is personal income, from the national income and product accounts. In fact, personal income is too small in some respects and too large in others. It does not include realized capital gains or pension benefits (which do not arise from new production, as does personal income, but rather from the exchange of existing assets). But personal income includes the incomes of nonprofit organizations (such as the interest income on university endowments) and of financial intermediaries (such as the interest income on life insurance company and pension fund reserves). Thus comparisons of the tax base with personal income, while indicative, are not a precise measure of the state of the tax system.

Table 2 shows that from the time of the enactment of the Internal Revenue Code in 1954 to 1982 (the latest year for which data are available), income taxed at positive rates—that is, not including the zero-bracket amount— increased from 38.7 percent to 46.1 percent of personal income. From this measure, it would appear that leakages from the tax base have been reduced, making the income tax more uniform and fair. Unfortunately, several details in the data indicate the opposite.

The 7.9 percentage-point growth of the tax base as a percentage of personal income is more than accounted for by a net reduction of 13.4 percentage points in the portion of personal income shielded from tax by the personal exemptions and zero-bracket amounts. The exemptions and zero brackets provide nondiscriminatory relief to taxpayers, particularly those with lower incomes; their erosion over time probably signals an erosion of fairness.

In contrast, several more preferential exclusions from taxable income grew over the period. Itemized deductions in excess of the standard deduction or zero-bracket amount more than doubled as a percentage of personal income. Exclusions of nonwage labor income, which benefit some workers but not others, almost tripled. Tax credits, some of which constitute subsidies to particular taxpayers, also tripled as a fraction of personal income shielded from tax.

As was suggested earlier, these measures are only imperfect indicators of the perceived unfairness of the income tax. Most tax shelters reduce measured personal income, not the percentage of personal income subject to tax, and so are not highlighted by this methodology. The itemized deduction figure includes not only any manipulative deductions, but also extraordinary and burdensome medical expenses. The tax credits include the earned income credit for low-income working families with children as well as investment credits received by individuals (and the figures do not weigh the investment incentive value of that credit against its violation of any taxpayers' standards

TABLE 2

RECONCILIATION OF PERSONAL AND TAXABLE INCOME, 1954 AND 1982

(In Billions of Dollars)

	1954 Current Dollars	1954 Percentage of Personal Income	1982 Current Dollars	1982 Percentage of Personal Income	Change as Percentage of Personal Income
Personal income including capital gains[a]	$295.0	100.0%	$2605.9	100.0%	0.0%
Less:					
Transfers	11.4	3.9%	324.7	12.5%	8.6%
Untaxed labor income	5.8	2.0%	154.5	5.9%	4.0%
Capital gains exclusion[b]	2.4	0.8%	27.3	1.0%	0.2%
Other[c]	20.5	6.9%	80.1	3.1%	-3.9%
Equals:					
Adjusted Gross Income (Bureau of Economic Analysis)	254.9	86.4%	2,019.3	77.5%	-8.9%
Less:					
Gap[d]	25.7	8.7%	167.2	6.4%	-2.3%
Equals:					
Adjusted Gross Income (IRS)	229.2	77.7%	1,852.1	71.1%	-6.6%
Less:					
Nontaxable returns	19.5	6.6%	48.3	1.9%	-4.8%
Equals:					
AGI (Taxable returns)	209.7	71.1%	1,803.8	69.2%	-1.9%
Less:					
Exemptions	67.0	22.7%	191.4	7.3%	-15.4%
Standard deduction[e]	18.9	6.4%	217.9	8.4%	2.0%
Excess itemized deductions[e]	8.6	2.9%	169.7	6.5%	3.6%

TABLE 2 (continued)

(Billions of Dollars)

	1954 Current Dollars	1954 Percentage of Personal Income	1982 Current Dollars	1982 Percentage of Personal Income	Change as Percentage of Personal Income
Equals:					
Taxable income on taxable returns	115.2	39.1%	1,224.8	47.0%	8.0%
Less:					
Income offset by tax credits^f	0.9	0.3%	24.7	0.9%	0.6%
Equals:					
Income taxed at "nonzero" rates	114.3	38.7%	1,200.1	46.1%	7.3%
Total income tax	26.7	9.1%	277.6	10.7%	1.6%

SOURCES: Eugene Steuerle and Michael Hartzmark, "Individual Income Taxation 1947–1979," *National Tax Journal* (June 1981), pp. 161–162; U.S. Treasury, Internal Revenue Service, *Statistics of Income—1982, Individual Income Tax Returns*, (Washington, D.C.: U.S. Government Printing Office, 1984), unpublished IRS statistics; and Thae S. Park, "Personal Income and Adjusted Gross Income, 1980–1982," *Survey of Current Business*, vol. 62, no. 4, April 1984, pp. 53–55.

NOTE: Items may not add to totals because of rounding.

a. Includes realized capital gains reported on individual income tax returns.

b. Includes capital gains exclusion less amount of capital losses not deductible.

c. Includes income of nonpersons (e.g., nonprofit institutions and financial intermediaries), less income included in adjusted gross income (AGI) but not in personal income.

d. Includes Bureau of Economic Analysis (BEA) estimate of income earned but not reported on tax returns.

e. For 1954, amount of itemized deductions equal to the standard deduction is considered part of the standard deduction.

of fairness). Nonetheless, the results indicate that preferential leakages from the tax base have grown over the past thirty years.

Who Pays the Income Tax?

Although some people use extraordinary devices to avoid taxes and so attract public attention, most people claim only modest amounts of deductions and exclusions. What has happened to the tax burdens of these ordinary taxpayers? It is the many ordinary taxpayers at every income level, not the far fewer tax avoidance extremes, who determine the revenue collected by and the overall progressivity of the income tax. Departing from the existing pattern of tax burdens in any tax revision would raise the taxes of particular income groups, because if any one income group pays less tax, and the deficit is not to be widened, some other income group must pay more. So to avoid imposing needless pain, we must understand what is happening to the typical taxpayer. In the remainder of this chapter we present the available data on who pays the income tax and what changes have occurred since the adoption of the Internal Revenue Code of 1954.

Taxes and the Economy

Changes in tax burdens are not caused solely by changes in the tax law—although legislation has been frequent and significant over the past thirty years. Changes in the economy itself have interacted with the tax law to determine who pays the taxes. Two kinds of economic changes have affected the taxes that people have paid.

The first, widely recognized, was inflation. The price level (as measured by the Consumer Price Index) increased at annual average rates of 1.2 percent from 1954 to 1964, 4.6 percent from 1964 to 1974, and 7.7 percent from 1974 to 1984. As the recent rapid inflation increased taxpayers' nominal (but not real) incomes, it pushed them into higher tax rate brackets and eroded the value of their personal exemptions and deductions. As a result, taxes increased—but to different degrees at different income levels, depending on where each taxpayer stood among the tax rate brackets, and how each was affected by periodic tax cuts. Only tax bracket indexation, effective in 1985, has brought this process to a halt.

Most taxpayers are now painfully aware of this inflation-induced "bracket creep," but fewer realize that real economic growth can have a similar effect. Even without inflation, the steady growth of productivity and real incomes gradually pushes taxpayers into higher tax rate brackets and could eventually overwhelm the exemptions and standard deductions. Most people dislike the effects of inflation-induced bracket creep, but have given little thought to the acceptability of real "bracket climb." From a macroeconomic policy point of view, bracket climb causes growth in real tax revenues to exceed the real growth of the economy. In the macroeconomic literature, the more rapid growth in revenues has been called "fiscal drag," because it would tend to slow economic growth (through a conventional Keynesian deflation) unless it were offset through increased government spending or reduced taxes. In view of our current deficit crisis, we might appreciate this bracket climb in the short run for the modest additional revenue it yields. Over the long haul, however, we might prefer tax cuts to offset at least some of the bracket climb. Ultimately, the decision depends on the desired size of the public sector. For the extreme example, under the current tax law and in the far-distant future, even without inflation, most income would fall into the highest (50 percent) tax rate bracket; we probably would not want the federal sector spending nearly 50 percent of our national income.

Tax Burdens, 1954–1984

Because of the important effect of economic change on the level of tax liabilities, analysis of tax burdens over time must separate the effects of growth and inflation from those of explicit changes in the tax law. To get at this complex picture, we compare the tax liabilities of four-person husband-wife families with the median income (and multiples of it) over the post-1954 period. The median income increases from year to year through both inflation and real growth. This method avoids some pitfalls of a more common approach, comparing taxpayers with constant real incomes that change only for inflation. For example, if we were to compare a 1954 median-income family with another family that had the same real income in 1984, the latter would have less than half of the median real income in the later year—in effect, it would have missed out on all the real economic growth that took place over those thirty years. Comparing such families' taxes in 1954 and 1984 would not compare two similarly situated families, but rather two very dissimilar families. Comparing families with the median income in each year gives a better picture.[13]

These computations portray a family that claimed an average amount of deductions (taking account of the number of families that claimed the standard deduction) for its income level in each year but used no other tax preferences.

---

13. These comparisons are not intended to follow the same hypothetical family over this thirty-year period; rather, the figures show the taxes of *comparably situated* families in any two years. Similarly, there is no attempt to adjust for changes in typical family size or in timing of childbirth over time (which might make the typical four-person family older and richer by 1984).

Thus, this is a kind of "typical median-income family" whose taxes clearly reflect the basic structure of the tax system. It does not show the effect of the less frequently used tax preferences that enable some families to pay less than the typical amount of tax. This factor is discussed in more detail later in this chapter.

Table 3 shows that the tax burden on the median-income family as a percentage of its income nearly doubled between 1954 and 1980, from 6.2

TABLE 3

TAX BURDENS ON FAMILIES AT MULTIPLES OF THE MEDIAN INCOME, 1954–1984
(Percentage)

Year	Multiple of the Median Income						
	0.25	*0.5*	*1*	*2*	*3*	*5*	*10*
1954	0	0	6.16	12.04	14.82	18.63	28.21
1955	0	0	6.76	12.44	15.22	19.25	29.24
1956	0	0	7.51	12.94	15.78	19.91	30.40
1957	0	0	7.71	13.20	15.72	20.42	30.72
1958	0	0	7.91	13.29	15.57	20.75	31.14
1959	0	1.04	8.40	13.24	15.94	21.42	31.83
1960	0	1.65	8.61	13.02	16.15	21.52	31.97
1961	0	2.10	8.81	13.20	16.34	24.90	32.52
1962	0	2.67	9.08	13.36	16.56	22.10	32.81
1963	0	3.44	9.40	13.63	17.05	22.87	34.00
1964	0	2.15	8.22	12.48	16.03	21.04	31.63
1965	0	2.54	7.86	11.98	15.36	20.41	30.88
1966	0	3.43	8.44	12.81	16.03	21.41	32.12
1967	0	4.05	8.84	13.07	16.43	22.13	32.95
1968	0	4.94	10.11	14.62	18.21	24.80	36.03
1969	0	5.80	10.98	15.65	19.38	26.26	36.17
1970	0	6.02	10.09	14.67	18.29	25.03	33.89
1971	0	4.58	9.43	14.11	17.93	24.73	33.79
1972	0	4.00	9.20	14.03	18.11	25.24	34.22
1973	0	4.98	9.79	14.83	19.10	26.71	36.19
1974	0	5.69	10.17	15.34	19.92	27.74	37.11
1975	− 10.00	2.67	9.56	15.21	20.17	28.11	37.76
1976	− 9.75	3.83	9.94	16.10	21.16	29.34	39.39
1977	− 8.17	2.81	10.17	16.77	22.47	30.23	40.26
1978	− 6.55	4.03	11.02	17.77	23.92	31.51	41.55
1979	− 9.30	4.60	11.16	17.60	23.92	31.77	41.15
1980	− 8.64	5.40	11.60	18.34	24.67	32.44	41.43
1981	− 7.45	6.29	12.26	19.17	24.93	31.89	40.67
1982	− 6.72	5.93	11.26	17.58	22.58	29.02	34.96
1983	− 5.82	5.94	10.51	16.41	21.05	27.01	33.93
1984	− 4.97	6.03	10.29	15.99	20.53	26.05	33.30

SOURCE: Computed by the author.

percent to 11.6 percent. More than half of that growth had occurred by 1963, however. The Kennedy-Johnson tax cuts reduced the median-income family's burden about halfway back to the 1954 level, but inflation and rapid real growth pushed it to 11.0 percent (including the Vietnam War surtax) by 1969.

The years since 1969 have seen continued and accelerated inflation, slower real growth, and numerous tax cuts to relieve bracket creep. The Tax Reform Act of 1969 cut the median burden to 9.2 percent in 1972, when fully phased in, but further inflation and growth—even with three tax cut bills—let the burden climb to 11.0 percent in 1978. Continued bracket creep outweighed a tax cut passed in late 1978 to leave the tax burden at 11.6 percent in 1980.

The Economic Recovery Tax Act of 1981 (ERTA) responded to this increase. ERTA included across-the-board cuts of 1.25 percent in the tax rates for 1981, about 10 percent as of 1982, about 19 percent as of 1983, and about 23 percent as of 1984.[14] As of 1982, the maximum marginal tax rate was set at 50 percent, instead of 70 percent—both a larger and an earlier rate reduction for the taxpayers with the highest incomes.[15] ERTA also indexed the tax rate brackets and personal exemptions for inflation effective in 1985, and established numerous other incentive and subsidy provisions. The modest 1981 rate cut installment failed to compensate the median-income taxpayer fully for inflation, but thereafter tax burdens were cut in real terms. By 1984, the median-income taxpayers paid about 10.3 percent of their income in tax, or not much less than in 1978.

Increasing Progressivity

Why should the burden of median-income taxpayers have increased so much over the 1954-1980 period? The total yield of the individual income tax increased only from 9.2 percent to 11.6 percent of personal income (as measured by the national income and product accounts) from 1954 to 1980, but the burden on median-income taxpayers almost doubled. The answer is that the increase in the burden on median-income taxpayers was part of a long-

---

14. Most taxpayers (those who are employees) received the cash from these tax rate cuts in the form of withholding reductions of 5 percent on October 1, 1981, a further 10 percent on July 1, 1982, and a final 10 percent on July 1, 1983—cumulatively the same 23 percent reduction as that in the statutory marginal rates.

15. The Tax Reform Act of 1969 limited the highest marginal tax rate on labor income for taxpayers with a large amount of income from labor (as opposed to property) to 50 percent.

term shift toward a more progressive income tax, in which inflation, real growth, and the structure of the income tax all played important roles.[16]

Part of this shift was a reduction in the tax burden on the lowest-income taxpayers. It began with the 1964 tax cut, which included a substantial increase in the minimum standard deduction. The larger standard deduction saved some taxpayers from the paperwork burden of itemizing their deductions, but more notably it cut the taxes of the lowest-income taxpayers who were not likely to itemize in any event. This step began a practice of making families below the official poverty line totally free of income tax. Further increases in the personal exemptions and the standard deduction over the late 1960s and the 1970s were justified by this purpose, and a general tax credit was used for a time in the late 1970s to the same effect. When revenues were short this purpose was temporarily ignored, as it has been since 1978.

In 1975 a negative tax of sorts was devised for low-income families with children. The refundable earned-income tax credit equaled 10 percent of income from labor up to a maximum $400 credit, and any excess of the credit over tax otherwise owed was paid to the family in cash. The credit is phased out as income increases. It was increased to a maximum of $500 in the 1978 tax cut bill.

For the economy as a whole, these tax cuts of the late 1960s and the 1970s compensated for inflation, leaving total income taxes a roughly constant share of personal income; but the impact of the cuts across the population was uneven. Through the increased exemptions and standard deductions and the new earned-income tax credit, taxes were reduced more in percentage terms for people with modest incomes.[17] But the tax cuts did not significantly

---

16. Income tax progressivity can be measured in several different ways, as explained in Richard A. Musgrave and Tun Thin, "Income Tax Progression, 1929-1948," *Journal of Political Economy*, vol. 56, December 1948, pp. 498-514. As the discussion that follows in the text makes clear, the U.S. income tax was made unambiguously more progressive several times between 1954 and 1980 through increased relief for people with low incomes. Nonetheless, the long-term effect of real growth and inflation on progressivity could be debated. One could argue that real growth has no effect on progressivity but merely shifts taxpayers further up a constant tax function. One could also argue that inflation would decrease progressivity in the far-distant future, pushing all taxpayers into the highest bracket, so that we would have, in effect, a flat tax. In the context of the 1954-1984 period, however, both inflation and real growth pushed the income group with the largest number of taxpayers, those with middle incomes, up the marginal-tax-rate schedule into the income range where tax rates increased most steeply. For that reason, those taxpayers' liabilities and marginal rates increased rapidly from year to year. It is this practical measure of progressivity, rather than a theoretical measure, to which this discussion refers.

17. This is a perfectly proper result in the context of inflation. Nontaxable persons whose income is increased to a taxable level because of inflation should get a 100 percent tax cut to hold them harmless from that inflation.

slow the effects of the bracket creep and bracket climb that pushed moderate-income taxpayers into higher rate brackets. Only in 1978 was a tax cut focused on the tax rate structure, and its effects were immediately overwhelmed by three years of rapid inflation.

The effects of these legal changes can be seen in table 3. Families at one-quarter of the median income were nontaxable over the entire 1954-1984 period, and since 1975 they have received negative taxes.[18] Families at one-half of the median income grew into taxability between 1954 and 1963, but their taxes were kept very low over the entire period. Their tax burden increased by less than one percentage point between 1963 and 1978, increasing since that time by two points, to about 6 percent.

In contrast, tax burdens for those above the median income increased sharply.[19] The tax burden at twice the median income increased by 6.3 percentage points from 1954 to 1980 (to more than 18 percent), in contrast to the 5.4 percentage points at the median (to less than 12 percent). At three times the median income, the increase was almost ten percentage points (to about 25 percent), and at five and ten times the median, it was more than thirteen percentage points (to about 32 and 41 percent respectively). It was at these higher income levels that taxpayers climbed up the steepest part of the tax rate schedule.

Table 3 confirms this shift toward greater progressivity by also showing how the tax burden increased as income increased in any given year. It is evident that taxes increased much more steeply with income in 1980 than in the 1950s or 1960s, with negative taxes at the lowest income level and significantly higher taxes at and above the median income.

Marginal Tax Rates

Table 4 shows data analogous to those in table 3, but for *marginal* tax rates rather than for the *average* tax burden. The marginal tax rate is the rate

---

18. Families below the median income are assumed to claim the standard deduction, to obtain all their income from labor, and to claim the earned-income tax credit (when in effect). Although such a family is typical of families at this income level who pay income taxes, it is less typical of all families at this income level, most of whom receive some income in the form of nontaxable government transfers.

19. Families above the median-income level are assigned the average itemized deductions claimed at each income level. The maximum tax provision for earned income, which limited the tax rate on labor income to 50 percent from 1971 through 1981, is assumed not to apply. These results show the tax liabilities of typical upper-income taxpayers. They do not portray the extent to which some taxpayers reduce their measured income for tax purposes through tax shelters or other devices. Nonetheless, the stated tax burdens measure the tax that such taxpayers would pay if they did not shelter their incomes, and thus may indicate the incentive for these taxpayers to shelter their income.

TABLE 4

MARGINAL TAX RATES ON FAMILIES AT MULTIPLES OF THE MEDIAN INCOME, 1954–1984
(Percentage)

	Multiple of the Median Income						
Year	0.25	0.5	1	2	3	5	10
1954	0	0	20.00	22.00	26.00	34.00	50.00
1955	0	0	20.00	22.00	26.00	34.00	53.00
1956	0	0	20.00	22.00	26.00	34.00	56.00
1957	0	0	20.00	22.00	26.00	34.00	56.00
1958	0	0	20.00	22.00	26.00	38.00	56.00
1959	0	20.00	20.00	22.00	26.00	38.00	59.00
1960	0	20.00	20.00	22.00	30.00	38.00	59.00
1961	0	20.00	20.00	22.00	30.00	38.00	59.00
1962	0	20.00	20.00	22.00	30.00	43.00	59.00
1963	0	20.00	20.00	26.00	30.00	43.00	62.00
1964	0	16.00	18.00	23.50	27.00	37.50	56.00
1965	0	14.00	17.00	22.00	28.00	39.00	53.00
1966	0	14.00	19.00	22.00	28.00	39.00	55.00
1967	0	15.00	19.00	22.00	28.00	42.00	55.00
1968	0	15.00	20.43	26.88	34.40	48.38	59.13
1969	0	19.20	20.90	27.50	35.20	49.50	63.80
1970	0	16.80	19.48	25.63	32.80	49.20	59.45
1971	0	15.00	19.00	25.00	36.00	48.00	58.00
1972	0	15.00	19.00	28.00	36.00	50.00	60.00
1973	0	16.00	19.00	28.00	39.00	50.00	62.00
1974	0	16.00	22.00	28.00	39.00	53.00	62.00
1975	− 10.00	26.00	22.00	32.00	42.00	53.00	62.00
1976	10.00	17.00	22.00	32.00	45.00	53.00	64.00
1977	10.00	16.00	22.00	36.00	45.00	55.00	66.00
1978	10.00	17.00	25.00	36.00	48.00	55.00	66.00
1979	0	16.00	24.00	37.00	49.00	59.00	68.00
1980	0	16.00	24.00	43.00	49.00	59.00	68.00
1981	12.50	17.78	23.70	42.46	48.39	58.26	67.15
1982	12.50	16.00	22.00	39.00	44.00	50.00	50.00
1983	12.50	15.00	23.00	35.00	44.00	48.00	50.00
1984	12.50	14.00	22.00	33.00	42.00	49.00	50.00

SOURCE: Computed by the author.

in the highest bracket the taxpayer reaches, rather than the average of the total tax over all the taxpayer's income. In other words, the marginal rate is the tax that would be due if the taxpayer earned one extra dollar of income. The marginal rate is always higher than the average rate for taxpaying returns, because some of the taxpayer's income is not taxed at all through exemptions and deductions, and other income is taxed in lower tax rate brackets.

Table 4 shows that the effect of bracket creep and bracket climb, and the resulting increased progressivity of the tax system, were, if anything, more pronounced in terms of marginal tax rates than average tax burdens. The marginal rate for taxpayers at one-half of the median income increased only two percentage points from 1965 to 1980, held in check largely by increases in exemptions and deductions (as well as by the 1978 law's rate changes). In contrast, the median taxpayer's marginal rate increased by seven percentage points over the same period. At higher income levels, the increases were striking; at twice and at three times the median, twenty one points; at five times the median, twenty points; and at ten times the median, fifteen points.

Taxpayers perceive increased tax burdens in terms of the dollars in their wallets. Increased marginal tax rates are perceived more as government intrusion upon taxpayers' economic decisions—whether to work overtime, to save, to borrow, or to buy a house, for example. Because marginal tax rates increased, taxpayers had greater reason to seek out and use tax deductions and exclusions, or even to conceal income. Such actions narrow the tax base, reduce government revenue, and erode popular respect for the income tax.

Other Tax Preferences

The figures presented thus far show the effects of changes in the tax rate structure, typical deductions, and the economy on the tax burdens of typical families. The major limitation of these data is that they do not show the full effect of preferential tax provisions or manipulation that might make the tax system more or less progressive than it appears in the figures. In addition, changing patterns in use of preferences or shelters may alter the trend of progressivity.

A better indicator of actual changes in income tax burdens would be "tax after all tax preferences as a percentage of true income." The ideal income measure would include all forms of income, whether subject to tax or not. The actual tax relative to true income would be the correct measure of the burden of the income tax on families.

Unfortunately, such a true measure of income is unattainable. The major roadblock is that many forms of income are never observed in a reliable and quantifiable way. For the most part, estimates of tax burdens and incomes must be confined to information that is reported on tax returns, and untaxed incomes either are not reported or are sheltered by accelerated or preferentially large business expense deductions. But it is possible to move part way toward a measure of the tax burden on true income by making the typical families in our example somewhat less typical—that is, by showing how their taxes and measured incomes would change if they made greater use of the tax preferences shown on tax returns. Over the time span examined here, such preferences (generally used by a minority of taxpayers) include a credit or exclusion for part of corporate dividends received, the exclusion for part of long-term capital gains, tax credits for investment and child care expenses, and a number of minor provisions. All these provisions have some rationale, but they also make the tax base depart from a comprehensive measure of income that would be most evenhanded for tax purposes.

In fact, computation of tax liabilities and incomes with these preferences shows that their effect has been growing over the past three decades. This finding accords with the federal government's measure of tax revenue lost because of tax expenditures, which has grown significantly both in terms of the number of such provisions and their revenue cost.[20] The data also suggest that these tax preferences benefit upper-income taxpayers most.

These conclusions are documented by assuming (1) that the typical families used their proportionate share of the tax credits claimed in their income groups and therefore paid lower taxes, and (2) that they used their share of the tax exclusions and therefore had higher incomes than was assumed in the baseline computations. Table 5 shows that measured tax burdens in 1954 would not be substantially different if tax preferences were included; the median-income family would pay only about 0.1 percentage point less. The effect of the preferences grows with income, however, reducing taxes by about 1.4 percentage points at ten times the median.

By 1980, however, the effect of the measured preferences is almost six times as great. The median-income family using its share of the tax preferences

TABLE 5

TAX BURDENS ON FAMILIES AT MULTIPLES OF THE MEDIAN INCOME WITH AND WITHOUT TAX PREFERENCES, 1954 AND 1980
(Percentage)

	Multiple of the Median Income						
Year	0.25	0.5	1	2	3	5	10
	Without Tax Preferences						
1954	0	0	6.16	12.04	14.82	18.63	28.21
1980	−8.64	5.40	11.60	18.34	24.67	32.44	41.43
	With Tax Preferences						
1954	0	0	6.10	11.96	14.49	17.85	26.83
1980	−8.64	5.00	11.24	17.17	22.04	26.91	32.78

SOURCE: Computed by the author.

20. Joint Committee on Taxation, *Estimates of Federal Tax Expenditures for Fiscal Years 1984-1989* (Washington, D.C.: U.S. Government Printing Office, November 9, 1984), table 1, pp. 9-16.

pays 0.6 percentage point less, and the family at ten times the median income pays about 7.4 percentage points less.

These data clearly have some limitations. The list of tax preferences whose effects are measured is incomplete; for example, tax-free employer-paid fringe benefits for workers are not included, nor are most outright tax shelters that reduce measured income. These other leakages from the tax base, for which reliable tax return data do not exist, might easily affect the overall picture if they could be included. Moreover, the definition of tax preferences chosen here might be controversial; average amounts of itemized deductions are not considered preferences, and all statutory adjustments to income and tax credits are.

Nonetheless, there is a broad message from these results. The federal income tax is progressive, even if some of the most important preferential tax provisions are considered. But the influence of tax preferences on the tax system is growing, and tentative evidence suggests that these preferences are tilted toward taxpayers in the upper-income brackets. This fact can affect both our assessment of the fairness of the current system and our decision of whether and how it should be changed.

Were All These Changes Fair?

From 1954 through 1980, therefore, the distribution of the tax burden shifted dramatically toward greater progressivity. This change was driven partly by legislation, and partly by the interaction of the existing progressive tax structure with real economic growth and (especially) rapid inflation. In 1981, tax rates were cut proportionally across-the-board. Were all these changes fair?

This question can best be considered by looking separately at taxpayers below, at, and above the median-income level, and seeing how they were affected by the drift of the tax burden over these years. But once more, fairness is subjective, and so this question has no single answer.

Who Should Pay?

Low-Income Taxpayers. The treatment of taxpayers below the median income was changed explicitly over the last thirty years. First, the introduction of a substantial minimum standard deduction in the 1964 law began the practice of completely exempting people below the official poverty line. Then, in 1975, the enactment of the earned-income credit established a new (some might say higher) standard: that working low-income families should receive an actual subsidy, to offset their Social Security payroll taxes and defray their other living costs. So there has been a new movement in the past twenty years toward lifting the income tax burden from low-income families.

This new movement probably makes sense. Eliminating the income tax of the poor has an efficiency as well as a humanitarian rationale. It would be costly for the IRS to sift through millions of tax returns of low-income people who would pay only token amounts of tax, especially if those taxpayers had some difficulty filing their returns correctly. There is some public support for the notion, however, that everyone, no matter how poor, should pay at least a token amount of tax;[21] perhaps the Social Security payroll tax and state and local sales taxes would satisfy this standard, however.

The earned-income tax credit took the exemption of poor people one step further by adding an actual subsidy. That step is probably more controversial. The credit is extremely complex for taxpayers to understand. Without substantial extra paperwork on the part of the employer, the credit is received as a lump sum after the tax year is over and the tax return is filed, so it is not help with ongoing living costs. And families that have such low income that they legally need not file a return, might neglect to claim the credit. Nonetheless, the earned-income tax credit fills an important gap in an income support system that focuses mostly on nonworking families—especially considering the Social Security payroll tax that low-income working families have to pay.

The data show that the earned-income credit, as well as the personal exemptions and zero-bracket amounts that protect the poor and the near-poor, have been badly eroded by the rapid inflation since 1975. The lack of attention to this problem in the late 1970s was serious enough, but by 1981, the effects of inflation on these families were well known. Yet the Reagan administration, in proposing its very large tax cut, and the Congress, in legislating it, chose to ignore the problem. As a result, there has been a steady increase in the income tax burden on low-income families. Thus, the 1981 tax law can be judged unambiguously, at least by our post-1964 standards, to have been unfair to the poor; taxes of sub-median-income families have gone up since 1980, while the taxes of the better-off went down. The indexing of the exemptions and the tax brackets beginning in 1985, included in the 1981 tax law, does not solve this problem. The indexation provision makes no correction for the inflation between 1978 and 1984, and it does not increase the earned-income credit at all.

---

21. The Roper Organization, *Third Annual Tax Study*, p. 25, shows a narrow majority of 56 percent to 41 percent agreeing that the poor should pay no tax.

Middle-Income Taxpayers. The burden on median-income taxpayers crept steadily upward over the period. In part, this is a reflection of the increase in the total income tax burden; for the total income tax take to go up significantly, median-income taxpayers had to pay more. This increase in tax burdens was a response to the rising deficits of the late 1970s, when the energy shocks and resultant slow economic growth dragged the federal budget into larger deficits. But by 1980, there was universal agreement that tax burdens had gotten out of hand, and so a 1981 tax cut was inevitable.

Like low-income taxpayers, families around the median-income level were relatively shortchanged (though to a lesser degree) by the 1981 tax law's failure to adjust the personal exemptions and standard deductions for the past inflation. This was apparent in table 3, for example, which shows a smaller tax cut at the median income than at five to ten times that level.

Another aspect of the question, however, is real growth. Between 1954 and 1980, the median income increased in real terms by more than 74 percent before taxes, and by more than 63 percent even after the increased tax burden; the inflation-adjusted purchasing power of median-income people increased substantially, and so their ability to pay clearly increased.

Upper-Income Taxpayers. As the figures show, the increases in tax burdens above the median-income level through 1980 were the most striking. If taxes had to increase, surely some of the burden should properly have rested on the taxpayers with the greatest ability to pay. But should their tax burdens have increased so much? There is no simple and definite answer.

As was noted earlier, taxpayers with incomes of three or more times the median had increases in their tax burdens, expressed as percentages of their incomes, about twice as large as the median-income family's. Thus, the well-to-do picked up more of the fiscal slack in absolute terms than did the typical taxpayer.[22]

The weakness in this viewpoint is that the 1980 and earlier tax laws could achieve their heavy tax burdens on the very well off (almost 38 percent at ten times the median income in 1975, and more than 41 percent at that income level in 1980) only through high marginal tax rates—up to 70 percent in 1975 and 1980. Generally, people think of fairness in terms of the tax

---

22. The maximum tax rate of 50 percent on labor income, enacted in 1969, restrained this increase in the tax burden of upper-income taxpayers. For families at ten times the median income, with all their income from labor, for example, the tax burden increased from 28.21 percent in 1954 to only 35.21 percent in 1980, instead of to the 41.43 percent paid by families with most or all of their income from capital. However, just as such families were hurt less by economic developments through 1980, so they benefited less from the tax cuts of 1981—the reduction of the highest marginal rate from 70 percent to 50 percent provided no new benefit for taxpayers already using the 50 percent maximum rate on labor income.

burden—the tax paid as a percentage of income. By 1981, however, people had come to think of high *marginal* tax rates as unfair; the federal government, this attitude seemed to hold, should not be a senior partner, asking more than half of the last dollar of anyone's income. It is no mystery how this attitude arose; many more people were being inflated into the highest tax rate brackets, and untold others hoped to reach those income levels someday.[23]

If this standard of fairness is now widely and strongly held, it will limit actual tax burdens. Now that marginal rates do not exceed 50 percent, there is no way that the income tax can impose late-1970s-style 40 percent tax burdens on any families but those with the very highest incomes. Thus, regaining the progressivity of the 1975 or 1980 tax laws would require reinstalling Uncle Sam as a senior partner of upper-income families. Nonetheless, even at the lower 1984 marginal rates, families at ten times the median income have almost exactly the same tax burden that they did in 1965, just after the Kennedy tax cuts.

So there are no definitive answers to the fairness of the tax evolution of the 1960s and 1970s, or of the 1981 tax cuts. The criteria point in different directions, and in the end any judgment is subjective. But people who maintain that they liked the tax law better "before 1981" have a further judgment to make: at what time before 1981?

Which Tax Law Was Right?

Clearly, the effect of the tax system changed substantially from 1954 to 1980. The distribution of the tax burden in any given year was different from the distribution in any other, even between years when the law did not change. So if any one year had the right distribution, it follows that every other year was wrong.[24]

---

23. It is also worth considering how people perceive the tax system. The figures shown here arise from a detached view of the world, looking at median-income-level taxpayers year after year. Actual taxpayers see things differently; they tend to start near the bottom of the economic ladder and climb upward as their careers progress. From this viewpoint, the increase in progressivity in the tax system was even greater than suggested here. For example, families at the median-income level in 1965 paid about 7.9 percent of their income in tax and were in the 20 percent marginal rate bracket; by 1980, they paid 11.6 percent and were in the 24 percent bracket. But an actual family that climbed from the median-income level to double the median-income level by 1980 would have seen its tax burden more than double to about 18.3 percent and its marginal rate more than double to 43 percent. From this viewpoint, the income tax would seem even more intrusive, and a limit on marginal rates at 50 percent—given some optimism about future income growth—even more attractive.

24. This is true unless our standards of fairness changed over time, perhaps in response to changes in real income levels.

The ideal distribution might be judged to be any of the following: (1) the 1954 law itself; (2) the Kennedy-Johnson tax law (in its first year of full effect in 1965); (3) the 1975 law, at the introduction of the earned-income tax credit; or (4) the 1980 law, the last year prior to the 1981 tax cuts. Let us compare how those tax laws would have distributed the 1984 burden, assuming that they were adjusted precisely for subsequent inflation. Table 6 does just that.

Two things stand out in this comparison. First, the later tax laws (except the one for 1984) become increasingly progressive in their overall distribution of the tax burden. From this perspective, it is the 1980 tax law that is the extreme case. The 1984 law, except in its handling of the income extremes, is more a step back to the laws of the 1950s and the 1960s than a move in a radically new direction. And second, the retreat from the 1975 tax relief for low-income families is apparent. Tax laws after that point provide lower subsidies and impose higher taxes on families below the median income.

Thus, people who dislike the effect of the 1981 tax cuts must recognize that the law it replaced was a post-1954 extreme, more progressive in its distribution of the tax burden (apart from the erosion of low-income relief) than any law of the preceding twenty five years, reached as much through drift as conscious choice. Without the marginal rates over 50 percent, which were removed with general approval, no substitute for the 1981 tax cuts could perpetuate the progressivity of the 1980 tax law.

The Income Tax and Other Taxes

As if these federal income tax considerations had not sufficiently muddied the waters, there are broader issues that make tax progressivity even more confusing and controversial. Since 1954, the payroll tax for Social Security

TABLE 6

TAX BURDENS ON FAMILIES AT MULTIPLES OF THE MEDIAN INCOME UNDER INDEXED HISTORICAL TAX LAWS, 1984

(Percentage)

Tax Law	Multiple of the Median Income						
	0.25	0.5	1	2	3	5	10
1954	0	5.04	10.76	15.61	19.17	25.08	37.90
1965	0	4.42	9.07	12.95	16.72	22.64	33.39
1975	− 10.00	2.63	9.85	14.74	19.21	26.34	35.56
1980	− 8.80	5.21	11.70	17.93	23.86	30.86	39.97
1984	− 4.97	4.10	9.75	15.78	21.06	26.05	33.30

SOURCE: Computed by the author.

has been our fastest growing tax, increasing from 10.3 percent to 36.5 percent of federal revenue. As a proportional tax on wages that has no exemption or deduction and applies to only a limited amount of wages, the payroll tax is regressive and bears relatively much more heavily on the typical worker than does the income tax. This situation might suggest that the income tax should be adjusted to compensate. But payroll taxes in effect ''buy'' a right to a retirement income that is computed through a formula that benefits low-income workers disproportionately. Should the income tax be modified to compensate for changes in the payroll tax, or should the Social Security system, both taxes and transfers, be considered completely separate? There is no simple answer.

Table 7 shows effective tax rates in selected years including both the income tax and the Social Security payroll tax. (Married couples are assumed here to have one earner. If both spouses were in the labor force, payroll taxes at income levels above the median would be higher.) Including the payroll tax increases the burdens on low- and middle-income taxpayers significantly more than considering the income tax alone. Families from one-half to twice the median income had their tax burdens increase by ten percentage points from 1954 to 1980; for the median-income family, this is an increase of 125 percent.

Including the payroll tax also changes the perspective on the 1981 tax cuts. By 1984, families at one-quarter of the median income were paying net positive taxes. Payroll tax increases eat significantly into the 1981 tax cuts of families from about one to three times the median income; only families above that level emerge with substantial tax cuts relative to 1980. Nonetheless, families at ten times the median income still paid more of their income in tax in 1984 than they did in 1965, just after the Kennedy-Johnson tax cuts.

TABLE 7

TAX BURDENS ON FAMILIES AT MULTIPLES OF THE MEDIAN INCOME INCLUDING
SOCIAL SECURITY PAYROLL TAX, SELECTED YEARS, 1954–1984
(Percentage)

Tax Law	Multiple of the Median Income						
	0.25	0.5	1	2	3	5	10
1954	2.00	2.00	7.82	12.87	15.37	18.96	28.37
1965	3.63	6.17	10.24	13.17	16.16	20.88	31.12
1975	−4.35	8.32	15.22	17.44	21.03	27.44	36.13
1980	−2.51	11.53	17.97	21.65	26.42	32.51	40.90
1984	2.03	13.03	17.29	20.62	23.61	27.90	34.22

SOURCE: Computed by the author.

So how one views the changes in tax burdens since 1954 depends on one's view of the payroll tax: whether it is viewed as savings to provide for a retirement income or as just a tax to support a transfer program. The choice between these two views is subjective; there is no ironclad case for either one.

Like payroll taxes, state and local taxes have grown rapidly since 1954, increasing from 6.4 percent of GNP to about 10 percent. Although a disproportionate share of that increase came in state and municipal income and wage taxes, which tend to be more progressive than the others, state and local taxes as a whole are far less progressive than the federal income tax. Should the federal income tax compensate for the growth of less progressive state and local taxes? Again, the choice is far from obvious.

Finally, the revenue yield of the federal corporate income tax has declined significantly, from about 30 percent of total federal revenues in 1954 to about 9 percent in 1984. The most common assumption is that the federal income tax is borne by owners of corporate shares and of other capital, rather than by consumers or employees of corporations.[25] Because owners of corporate shares and capital in general tend to be better off than the rest of the population, the decline of the corporate tax has decreased the progressivity of the overall tax system.

Joseph A. Pechman has found that the 1981 individual income tax cuts, together with the shifts in the payroll tax, the corporate income tax, and state and local taxes, have made the total tax system less progressive than it was in the early to mid-1970s.[26] Nonetheless, as was suggested here, the lessons for federal income tax policy are far from clear. It is not obvious that the income tax should be adjusted to compensate in full for changes in other taxes. The insurance aspects of the Social Security system suggest that the payroll tax might be considered apart from the others. The corporate tax has declined in part because of a slowdown of corporate profits, and so increasing corporate tax revenues on this comparatively smaller base would be difficult. And states and localities can impose their taxes to have the distributional effects that they want, and so the federal government might not want to undo the chosen tax patterns of the states and localities.

---

25. The reason is that in competitive markets, owners of corporations cannot shift the corporate tax onto their customers or employees. There is some shifting onto owners of capital in the unincorporated sector, however, because some capital flows there to avoid the corporate tax, driving down the rate of return. Arnold C. Harberger, "The Incidence of the Corporation Income Tax," *Journal of Political Economy*, vol. 70, June 1962, pp. 215-40.

26. Joseph A. Pechman, *Who Pays the Taxes?* (Washington, D.C.: The Brookings Institution, 1985).

Conclusions

Absolute conclusions about income tax fairness are hard to come by. We know that the income tax has become a large part of most families' budgets and strongly influences the market value of their most important assets (that is, their homes). For these reasons, the income tax can be changed only with care.

We can say that large-scale tax manipulation and avoidance are unfair and offensive and should be stopped. Tax manipulation and sheltering are undertaken by only a small minority of taxpayers (if we exclude the widely used and more limited tax preferences for homeownership, saving in IRAs, and so on). But conspicuous manipulation is destructive because it challenges the integrity of the income tax, encouraging further manipulation and even outright evasion. Still, opposing manipulation does not answer the more fundamental tax policy questions that affect all taxpayers directly through the overall distribution of the burden.

Here, the choices are much more controversial. The income tax has changed over time through legislation and through its interactions with the economy. These changes have been the subject of heated debate, and will probably continue to be so throughout the foreseeable future. Although there is an apparent consensus for a progressive income tax, the degree of progressivity that we want cannot be determined scientifically; it is a matter of public choice, and people's opinions vary over a wide range. An examination of recent history reveals that the distribution of the tax burden has shifted significantly, so there is no obvious historical baseline to follow. Any fundamental tax restructuring must somehow achieve broad public support for one concrete interpretation of the proper distribution of the tax burden. That task will not be easy.

CHAPTER 3

MAKING THE TAX SYSTEM MORE EFFICIENT

The economy's performance during the 1970s was a major disappointment. Economic growth was not up to par, slowing the rise in standards of living and exacerbating social tensions. Some observers concluded that the tax system was the problem and that simple tax cuts or targeted tax incentives were the solution.

But the salient fact about the slowdown in growth is how little economists can explain. There is no obvious button that economic policy can push to speed growth; and the role of the tax system is particularly hard to assess. Apparent economic distortions caused by the tax system, though cause for some concern, have no strong connection with the short-run performance of the economy. And our recent experiments with tax policy have had little visible effect.

What Is Tax Efficiency?

Resources to Run the Tax System

The most straightforward measure of "tax efficiency" is the quantity of resources that must be devoted to compliance and administration. Some resources understandably must be absorbed. Our actual resource losses exceed the inevitable minimum, however, because our tax law is more complex than it needs to be, and thus soaks up an inordinate amount of taxpayer and administrator time. This important topic is discussed on its own terms in the next chapter.

The concept of efficiency discussed most often in the past decade was quite different. That topic was efficiency for the entire economy.

The Tax System and the Economy

Economic theory suggests that virtually any tax will cause at least some inefficiency. By shifting the relative rewards of economic activities (various investment and work alternatives) and the relative prices of different products, the tax system can induce people to change the decisions that they would have made in the absence of taxes. For the most part, taxpayers' unconstrained choices (the ones that they would make in a free and properly functioning marketplace, without the intervention of taxes) would result in their greatest well-being. Any departure from those choices imposes economic costs on individuals and society.

Nonetheless, many of these economic inefficiencies are quite subtle and they generally go unnoticed in the short run. The primary focus in recent years has been on a broader issue: the alleged tendency of taxes to reduce the supply of factors of production (labor and capital) and hence to reduce incomes and economic growth.

Any tax introduces a "wedge" that can discourage the taxed activity. We might expect people to work more hours as their wage becomes higher, but an income or wage tax reduces the take-home wage and thus can decrease the incentive to work and the supply of labor. Similarly, a tax on capital income can, by reducing the reward for saving, discourage it and hence reduce the supply of capital. The higher the tax, the greater the disincentive. This twisting of incentives is called the "substitution effect"; it is the focus of the "supply-side economics" that lay behind the 1981 income tax cuts.

The effects of taxes are ambiguous, however. If a tax on wages pushes a worker close to destitution, the worker may be induced to work harder. A better-off worker may use a tax cut to finance longer vacations, winding up with the same after-tax income and more free time. There can be analogous results for a tax on capital income. Taxpayers may respond to such a tax by saving more, because with the tax they would have to save more to provide for their retirement and other future needs. After a tax cut, taxpayers might save less (and therefore enjoy more consumption) because they would need less saving to accumulate the same ultimate amount of wealth. These effects are called "income effects"; they arise because a tax cut increases after-tax income, enabling taxpayers to buy more of both the taxed good or activity and all others as well.

A complete view of the incentive effects of taxation, including the income as well as the substitution effects, is needed to assess the effects of tax policy on recent as well as future economic performance. This requires a look at the performance of the economy and the paths of factor supply (that is, the supplies of labor and capital) over the post-World War II years, and especially at the experience since the 1981 tax cuts. It also requires a consideration of other important influences on work effort, saving, and investment.

The Slowdown in Economic Growth in the 1970s

Many people are aware of the slowdown in economic growth that occurred in the 1970s. The worldwide oil shock of 1973 sent the U.S. economy into a deep recession in 1974-1975, and economic growth for the next few years was hesitant. Capping off the decade was a second brief but deep recession in 1980. Output in the private business sector of the economy grew by 3.7 percent per year between 1948 and 1973, but growth slowed to an average of 2.2 percent between 1973 and 1981; other sectors behaved similarly (see table 8).

Yet there was an even deeper dimension to this slowdown. The growth of labor productivity—output per worker-hour—slowed even more sharply. From 1948 to 1973, output per hour in the private business sector grew an average of 3.0 percent per year. From 1973 to 1981, however, productivity growth slowed to 0.8 percent per year.

Growth in labor productivity is important because it measures the real increase in the standard of living of our labor force. When labor productivity grew 3.0 percent per year, workers could receive 3.0 percent per year wage increases, on average, without increasing their employers' costs per unit of output (and therefore without increasing prices). When growth in productivity slowed to 0.8 percent per year, slower real wage growth and faster inflation were the unhappy results.

TABLE 8

AVERAGE ANNUAL GROWTH OF OUTPUT AND LABOR PRODUCTIVITY,
SELECTED PERIODS, 1948–1981
(*Percentage*)

Period	Private Business		Private Nonfarm Business		Manufacturing	
	Output	Productivity	Output	Productivity	Output	Productivity
1948–1973	3.7	3.0	3.9	2.5	4.0	2.9
1973–1981[a]	2.2	0.8	2.1	0.6	1.2	1.5
1948–1981	3.3	2.4	3.4	2.0	3.3	2.6

SOURCE: U.S. Department of Labor, Bureau of Labor Statistics, *Trends in Multifactor Productivity, 1948–81*, Bulletin 2178 (Washington, D.C.: U.S. Government Printing Office, September 1983), tables 8–10, pp. 22–24.

a. The Department of Labor used productivity over the year 1973 as both the end point for the earlier period and the beginning point for the later period.

To increase real living standards, we must increase our rates of growth of output and productivity. According to one theory, the slowdown in growth has been caused by declines in the rates of growth of the supplies of labor and capital, which have been caused by the tax system. To assess this theory, one must understand what has happened to factor supply and how the tax system has affected this process.

Taxation and Factor Supply: The Record

Taxation potentially affects the supplies of both capital and labor. As was documented in the preceding chapter, taxpayers faced increasing tax rates over the past three decades, both in terms of the dollars they paid and their marginal tax rates, and so supply-side advocates might fear a reduction in factor supply as a result. But the record is by no means clear cut.

The Supply of Labor

Many economic and social factors affect people's work decisions. Choices with respect to marriage and childbearing can increase or decrease the size of the labor force at any given time. Retirement decisions, based on the labor market and on pension and Social Security rights, can lead mature workers to prolong or shorten their participation in the work force. Educational opportunities and rewards, and even slack demand for labor, can lead young people to postpone their first jobs in favor of more schooling. At the same time, simple demography alters the flows of persons into and out of the prime working years.

Against this backdrop, taxation plays an uncertain role. As was noted earlier, the theoretical effect of taxation on labor supply is ambiguous; higher tax rates (or other real wage reductions) reduce the reward to working (the substitution effect) and thus decrease work; but higher tax rates also reduce people's incomes (the income effect) and thus increase work. This theoretical ambiguity can be resolved only through empirical research. Until recent years, the consensus was that both the substitution effect and the income effect were quite small for primary workers in families, and that the two effects tended to nearly cancel each other out (leaving a small net inducement of tax cuts to increase work effort).[1] For secondary workers in families, however, the tax effect was believed to be stronger. More recent research has confirmed

---

1. See the various studies in Glen C. Cain and Harold W. Watts, eds., *Income Maintenance and Labor Supply* (Chicago: Rand McNally, 1973).

the greater sensitivity of secondary workers to tax rates while suggesting that the substitution and income effects for primary workers, though still nearly offsetting, could each be larger than was previously believed.[2] This finding leaves open at least the prospect that rising tax rates for much of the population, as over the late 1960s and 1970s, would significantly hold back labor supply.

A crude measure of labor supply, the percentage of the adult civilian population in the labor force (that is, either working or looking for work), can be used to search for any apparent effects of tax rates on labor supply. But this measure, shown in figure 5, shows no obvious income tax effect. Throughout the 1950s and 1960s, the percentage of adults in the labor force

FIGURE 5

ADULT CIVILIAN LABOR FORCE PARTICIPATION RATE, 1947–1984

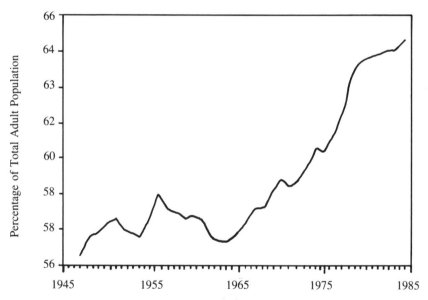

SOURCE: Council of Economic Advisers, *Economic Report of the President* (Washington, D.C.: U.S. Government Printing Office, February 1985), table B-29, p. 266.

---

2. If both the income and the substitution effects are greater, then a dollar tax cut that leaves taxpayers in the same marginal tax rate brackets would decrease labor supply more than previously would have been predicted. Conversely, a marginal tax rate cut that left dollar taxes unchanged would increase the labor supply more. Jerry A. Hausman, ''Labor Supply,'' in Henry J. Aaron and Joseph A. Pechman, eds., *How Taxes Affect Economic Behavior* (Washington, D.C.: The Brookings Institution, 1981), pp. 27-72.

remained relatively flat, at just under 60 percent, but in 1969 the percentage jumped over that mark. By 1974, the proportion was 61.3 percent; by 1981, it was 63.9 percent. In other words, the supply of labor veritably zoomed from its previous near-constancy at just about the time when inflation was pushing taxpayers into higher tax brackets and imposing larger tax burdens. Although other factors may have overwhelmed the tendency of the high marginal tax rates of the 1970s to depress the labor supply, the strength of the surge in the labor supply makes that seem unlikely. If anything, the higher tax burdens (and perhaps the economic slowdown) induced more work.

The growth of labor force participation in the 1970s is all the more remarkable because so much of it was accounted for by married women, who should have been the persons most deterred by higher tax rates. For example, if a family at twice the median-income level in 1975 was supported entirely by one spouse and the other contemplated working, the prospective worker would have faced a 32 percent marginal income tax rate on the first dollar of earnings (plus an additional 5.65 percent Social Security tax). An equivalent prospective worker in 1965 would have paid only 22 percent in income tax (and 3.625 percent in Social Security tax). So although the tax system, in retrospect, seems biased against two-earner married couples, married women joined the labor force anyway. In 1965, 37.6 percent of married women either worked or looked for work; in 1975, 42.3 percent did, and by 1981 the figure has risen to 48.6 percent.[3] Thus, at least in this basic measure of labor supply, tax effects are hard to find; and with the rapid growth of the labor supply, it is unlikely that economic growth was slowed by any shortage of labor.

The Supply of Capital

The growth in the supply of productive capital is more complex than the growth in the labor supply, in part because the capital formation process involves more actors. Funds are supplied in the financial markets by individuals, financial intermediaries, and other lenders; then those funds are invested by businesses. Tax policy can affect both parts of this process.

Taxation and Saving. Taxation affects household saving much as it does labor supply, imposing both income and substitution effects; so again, the net effect is indeterminate. A tax on the return to saving (or a fall in the real rate of return through higher inflation or lower interest rates) reduces that return (the substitution effect) and thus makes saving less attractive; but it also increases the amount of saving needed to accumulate any target level of

---

3. U.S. Council of Economic Advisers, *Economic Report of the President* (Washington, D.C.: U.S. Government Printing Office, February 1984), table B-30, p. 256.

future wealth (the income effect), thus making more saving necessary to prepare for retirement or achieve any other purpose. (At the same time, taxation affects total national saving in other ways—through its effect on the government's budget deficit, which is negative saving, and its influence on other savers, including financial institutions.)

The net effect of the federal income tax on household saving can only be determined empirically. Here again, the long-standing empirical result was that the effect of taxation was modest,[4] but some recent research has suggested a greater influence.[5] These claims have proved extremely controversial.[6] Some of the latest research, using data for the late 1970s that were not available for earlier work, again suggests that taxation has a relatively large influence; but the quantitative results do not explain significant changes in saving in the latter half of the 1970s.[7]

Household saving since World War II has fluctuated from about 4 percent to 7 percent of GNP, as shown in figure 6. Saving is influenced by the state of the economy, with greater saving in periods of high employment and reduced saving when unemployment is higher and people need to "dissave" (that is, to withdraw and spend prior savings) and borrow to maintain their standard of living. In recent recessions, however, tax cuts intended to stimulate the economy have resulted in temporary periods of increased saving (as taxpayers held their tax cuts for a time before spending them).

A recent puzzle in household saving is the drop in the saving rate starting in the mid-1970s. This drop is puzzling in part because it began with the economic recovery and decline of inflation that followed the 1974-1975 recession, and continued through the tax cuts of 1975, 1976, and 1978. It is episodes such as these that raise doubts about economists' capacity to understand, much less control, household saving behavior.

As was suggested earlier, household saving is only part of the story; private institutions also contribute to national savings. Figure 6 shows that total private saving has been more stable than household saving, varying only between about 15 percent and 18 percent over the post-World War II period.

---

4. Colin Wright, "Saving and the Rate of Interest," in Arnold C. Harberger and Martin J. Bailey, eds., *The Taxation of Income from Capital* (Washington, D.C.: The Brookings Institution, 1969), pp. 275-300.

5. Michael J. Boskin, "Taxation, Saving, and the Rate of Interest," *Journal of Political Economy*, vol. 86 (April 1978), part 2, pp. S3-S27.

6. E. Philip Howrey and Saul H. Hymans, "The Measurement and Determination of Loanable Funds Saving," in Joseph A. Pechman, ed., *What Should Be Taxed: Income or Expenditure?* (Washington, D.C.: The Brookings Institution, 1980), pp. 1-31.

7. Barry P. Bosworth, *Tax Incentives and Economic Growth* (Washington, D.C.: The Brookings Institution, 1984), pp. 79-84.

FIGURE 6

PERSONAL AND GROSS PRIVATE SAVING AS A PERCENTAGE OF GNP, 1947–1984

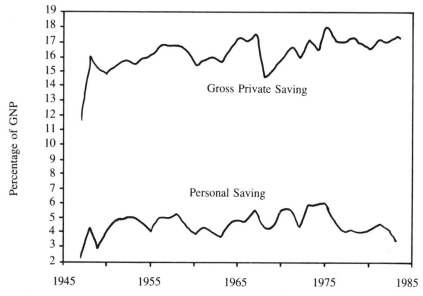

SOURCE: Council of Economic Advisers, *Economic Report of the President* (Washington, D.C.:
U.S. Government Printing Office, February 1985), table B-1, p. 232, and table B-
25, p. 262.

The stability of total private saving has been a subject of economic research
for some time.[8] One topic of research has been whether fluctuations in the
saving of households and institutions tend to offset each other to result in a
greater stability of total saving. For example, when households borrow or
dissave to maintain their standards of living in a recession, businesses may
save more because they do not need to add to productive capacity or inventories.[9] Perhaps because of such tendencies, total private saving shows a
smaller decline, relative to its long-term trend, than does household saving
in the late 1970s. The long-run stability of total private saving casts consid-

---

8. Edward F. Denison, "A Note on Private Saving," *Review of Economics and Statistics*,
vol. 40, August 1958, pp. 261-67.

9. George M. von Furstenberg, "Saving," in Henry J. Aaron and Joseph A. Pechman,
eds., *How Taxes Affect Economic Behavior* (Washington, D.C.: The Brookings Institution, 1981),
pp. 327-90, and comments, pp. 390-402.

erable doubt on the possibility of significantly increasing saving through tax policy.

Investment. The second half of the capital formation process is investment. In theory, businesses invest in productive capital as long as the return exceeds the cost; in so doing, they drive the return down until it equals cost. The cost of capital services includes depreciation, the cost of funds, and taxes. Over the post-World War II period, inflation has played an important role in determining the cost of capital, by driving up both interest rates and the effective tax rate on capital. Because the tax deduction for depreciation equals only the historical cost of an asset, inflation erodes the value of the tax deductions, and they fall short of the cost of replacing the asset. As a result, the actual tax burden is greater than it would be in the absence of inflation. Historically, the effective tax rate on business investments has shown wide swings owing to changes in both economic conditions and tax policy.[10]

Despite these fluctuations in the effective tax burden, investment has been relatively stable. Furthermore, if anything, investment has tended to rise slightly over the post-World War II years. Figure 7 shows that business investment has varied over a relatively narrow range from about 8 percent to 13 percent of GNP. There is no apparent drop in investment in the late 1970s to correspond to the drop in household saving. The visible fluctuations in investment correspond to cyclical influences; businesses plan to invest less during economic downturns and more when the economy is growing rapidly.

This stability of investment does not necessarily mean that investment behavior played no role in the slowdown in economic growth during the 1970s. Two factors are important. First, although investment was a relatively stable share of GNP over the past twenty years, the labor force was growing rapidly. It is not so much the size of the capital stock as the amount of capital each worker has to work with—the capital-labor ratio—that determines the productivity of the work force. Measured by that yardstick, the business-as-usual level of investment did not keep pace with labor force participation, and the capital-labor ratio grew more slowly in the 1970s.[11]

Second, the level of gross investment does not fully represent the change in the size of the capital stock. While businesses are investing in new assets, old assets are wearing out. Although new investment has been a relatively constant percentage of GNP, depreciation of the capital stock has been a growing percentage of GNP. This is caused by an increase in the share of

---

10. Charles R. Hulten and James W. Robertson, "Corporate Tax Policy and Economic Growth: An Analysis of the 1981 and 1982 Tax Acts," (Changing Domestic Priorities Working Paper, The Urban Institute, 1982).

11. Bosworth, *Tax Incentives and Economic Growth*, table 2-1, p. 24.

FIGURE 7

NONRESIDENTIAL INVESTMENT AS A PERCENTAGE OF GNP, 1947–1984

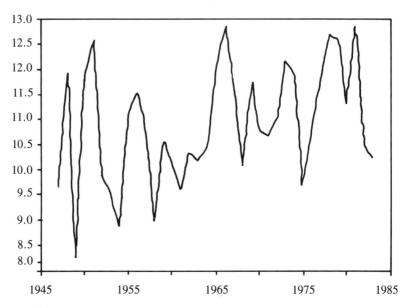

SOURCE: Council of Economic Advisers, *Economic Report of the President* (Washington, D.C.:
          U.S. Government Printing Office, February 1985), table B-1, p. 232.

short-lived assets in total investment. The effect of this shift on productivity
is uncertain.[12]

Accounting for Growth

So while labor supply has grown robustly, investment, though steady,
has not kept pace. Some economists have argued that a shortage of capital
formation was the major reason for the slowdown of productivity and economic growth in the 1970s.

---

12. The shift to shorter-lived assets makes the measured capital stock smaller, but short-
lived assets should add more to the productive capacity of the economy in the short run than do
long-lived ones. The reason is that a short-lived asset of a given cost must yield more output
per year over its life to be equally valuable to a long-lived asset of the same cost. Bosworth,
Tax Incentives and Economic Growth, p. 36.

A branch of economic research called "growth accounting" has attempted to determine the causes of economic growth.[13] The method is to measure the quantifiable influences on growth and productivity, and to associate the changes in those influential factors with changes in economic performance. Such studies have been performed on the experience of the 1970s, testing the allegation that growth was slowed by a shortage of capital formation, as well as other hypotheses. Unfortunately, however, this research leaves the causes of the slowdown in growth as a mystery.[14]

In one of the most recent efforts, Barry Bosworth concluded that of the 2.1 percentage-point reduction in the average annual rate of labor productivity growth in the nonfarm nonresidential business economy between the 1948-1967 period and the 1973-1980 period, as much as half could not be explained statistically. Only 0.1 to 0.2 percentage point of the productivity slowdown could be assigned to the differing rates of change in the capital-labor ratio between the two periods.[15]

The Bureau of Labor Statistics (BLS) has researched changes in productivity since 1948 and their causes. BLS also found a reduction of only 0.2 percentage point (out of a total productivity slowdown of 1.9 percentage points) attributable to slower growth of the capital-labor ratio in the private, nonfarm, business sector in the 1973-1981 period compared with the 1948-1973 period. However, BLS also separately investigated the manufacturing sector of the economy; it is in this sector that changes in investment in physical capital could have their greatest effect. In the manufacturing sector, the capital-labor ratio increased more rapidly in the 1973-1981 period than in the preceding twenty five years, and so there was no investment reduction to cause the slowdown in productivity growth.[16]

Conclusion

Investigations of the slowdown in economic growth and productivity during the 1970s, and of its causes, tend to be frustrating. There is little direct

13. Edward F. Denison, *Why Growth Rates Differ: Postwar Experience in Nine Western Countries* (Washington, D.C.: The Brookings Institution, 1967), is an early contribution.

14. Edward F. Denison, *Accounting for Slower Economic Growth: The United States in the 1970s* (Washington, D.C.: The Brookings Institution, 1979), is the most detailed such effort.

15. Bosworth, *Tax Incentives and Economic Growth*, table 2-4, p. 29.

16. U.S. Department of Labor, Bureau of Labor Statistics, *Trends in Multifactor Productivity, 1948-81*, Bulletin 2178 (Washington, D.C.: U.S. Government Printing Office, September 1983), p. 2. The slowdown in productivity is even more mysterious because it has touched every major industrialized country. This phenomenon raises doubts about the role of any influences that are alleged to be unique to the United States. John W. Kendrick, "International Comparisons of Recent Productivity Trends," in William Fellner, ed., *Essays in Contemporary Economic Problems: Demand, Productivity, and Population* (Washington, D.C.: American Enterprise Institute, 1981), p. 128.

association between measures of economic progress and identifiable causal factors. In particular, although insufficient capital formation appears at first glance to be an obvious drag on growth, the data tend not to support this view.

Furthermore, the data on labor force participation, saving, and investment themselves show much inertia. Some changes clearly reflect cyclical factors that are beyond the reach of long-term economic policy, while other changes, such as the slowdown in household saving in the late 1970s, show no apparent connection to any identifiable cause. In short, there is little suggestion from the record of the 1950s, 1960s, and 1970s of a likely significant increase in economic growth from any identifiable policy.

Experience of the 1980s—Prospects

Even though taxation and factor supply may not have been crucial elements in the economic slowdown of the 1970s, they still could contribute to more rapid growth now and in the future. If greater saving and capital formation were encouraged, for example, and if they did contribute to more rapid economic growth, it would matter little what had truly caused the slowdown of economic growth in the 1970s.

In that sense, the experience of the early 1980s and the prospects for future policy are closely linked. The Economic Recovery Tax Act of 1981, with its tax rate cuts for labor supply and saving and its more rapid depreciation for business investment, was the first post-World War II significant tax policy change targeted explicitly on economic growth.[17] Its success or failure will clearly indicate the potential of other tax policy changes to increase factor supply and economic growth in the future.

Unfortunately, no definitive judgment on the 1981 tax cuts is yet possible. It is reasonable, but optimistic, to forecast that the 1981 tax cuts would increase work effort, saving, and investment over the long run. Too little time has passed for those effects to be declared absent. So while any recent increases in factor supply could be cited as vindication of the tax-cut program, the program could not yet be judged a failure regardless of the indicators.

Even with this restriction, it is worthwhile to examine the data for signs of effects of the 1981 tax program, and for signs of the potential for tax policy to influence factor supply and growth.

---

17. The 1921, 1924, and 1926 tax cuts, strongly influenced by Treasury Secretary Andrew Mellon, might be counted as earlier experiments.

Labor Supply

The increases in labor force participation over the late 1960s and the 1970s were remarkable, especially in light of what would seem to be negative influences from taxation. Nonetheless, there is a point of saturation; only so many people can forsake postsecondary education, childrearing, and retirement to join (or remain in) the labor force. So the near constancy of adult civilian labor force participation since the 1981 tax cuts (see figure 5) should not be a surprise, especially considering the depth of the recession.

Given the extraordinary growth in the percentage of the adult population participating in the labor force since the 1960s, the scope for future tax policy to further increase that measure of participation is probably limited. Any effects are likely to be more subtle, such as increased hours of work by people who control their paid time on the job, or increased willingness of some people to work overtime or to accept more responsibility. Such effects would be measurable (if at all) only over a much longer period of time, and would have a more limited effect on the economy.

Capital Formation

Saving. Personal saving as a percentage of disposable personal income was 6.0 percent in 1980 and 6.7 percent in 1981, when the tax rate cuts were enacted. In 1982, personal saving fell to 6.2 percent, and further in 1983 to 5.0 percent, partially rebounding in 1984 to 6.1 percent—below the 1981 level.[18] So after the tax rate cuts, saving went down rather than up. This short-term experience is not a satisfactory indicator of the long-term effects of the tax reductions, because little time has passed and other factors (including the recession) could have overridden the effect of the policy change itself. Nonetheless, several other factors were favorable for an increase in saving. For example, real interest rates (after allowing for the rapid reduction of inflation) were at historical highs, providing their own inducement to save. Furthermore, the 1981 tax law provided an additional targeted savings incentive, the universal Individual Retirement Account (IRA), which allowed every worker to save $2,000 per year (or the worker's annual earnings, whichever was less) tax free until retirement. Finally, the cash from the tax cuts themselves was likely added to household saving, if only for a short time. So there is no favorable evidence on the 1981 tax cuts as a saving incentive.

---

18. Council of Economic Advisers, *Economic Report of the President* (Washington, D.C.: U.S. Government Printing Office, February 1985), table B-23, p. 260.

Investment. Nonresidential fixed investment (that is, investment in business plant and equipment) as a percentage of GNP ran at 11.7 percent in 1980, and 12.0 percent in 1981. After the 1981 tax cuts, investment fell to 11.4 percent in 1982 and 10.7 percent in 1983, before a partial recovery to 11.6 percent in 1984—still less than in 1980.[19]

The investment issue is even more cloudy than the personal saving issue. Investment falls in recessions, and so the effects of the tax reductions are hard to disentangle from normal cyclical fluctuations. Moreover, investment grew rapidly in 1984 (predictable in the later stages of a recovery). Despite this rebound, there are two enduring problems. One is that the 1984 increase in investment, though impressive in percentage terms, is really a moderate absolute increase from a depleted base. The 1982 and 1983 levels of business fixed investment as a percentage of GNP were quite low, and the 1984 figures are still below the long-term trend. Second, the very low investment of 1982 left a capital stock that was older on average. Depreciation figures suggest that new investment is quite low by historical standards relative to the wearing out of our existing capital stock (although this relationship is somewhat overstated because of the shift toward shorter-lived assets, as was explained earlier). Private nonresidential fixed investment net of depreciation was 2.9 percent of GNP in 1980 and 3.1 percent in 1981, but only 2.0 percent of GNP in 1982 and 1.5 percent in 1983 before recovering to 2.9 percent in 1984—no better than the 1980 level.[20] So although investment incentive effects of the 1981 tax cuts cannot be written off, the alleged benefits are yet to appear in any demonstrable form.

Prospects

The foregoing analysis suggests that labor supply was not a constraint on the growth of the economy in recent years. In fact, the growth of the work force has been so rapid that it raises real questions about the potential of tax policy to increase it further. Instead, appeals for tax changes targeted on growth tend to put their emphasis on capital formation.

Saving. Theory and history suggest that the level of national saving will be hard to budge through the individual income tax, and our current pattern of saving argues that it will be even harder. As is apparent from figure 6, much of gross private saving (79.3 percent in 1983) is done by corporations and through private pension plans;[21] corporate saving would be little influ-

---

19. Ibid., table B-1, p. 237.
20. Ibid., table B-15, p. 250.
21. U.S. Department of Commerce, *Survey of Current Business*, vol.64, no. 7, July 1984, table 5.4, p. 63.

enced by changes in the individual income tax, and pension plans are already tax-favored. Thus, the individual income tax has leverage on only a small fraction of total saving, and any percentage increase in household saving will add much less in percentage terms to total private saving.

Investment. There is also doubt as to just how much difference it would make if the United States did save more. To raise domestic productivity, saving would have to be devoted to business capital formation in the United States; but capital markets are increasingly international. In 1983 and 1984, foreign financial flows into the United States, largely attracted by high U.S. interest rates (as was suggested in chapter 1), were unprecedentedly large. If U.S. saving increased, reducing U.S. interest rates, some of that increase in saving would be offset by reduced inflows of foreign funds.

Another recent phenomenon is the growth of U.S. investment in financial and real assets overseas, as foreign firms grew to be competitive and U.S. investors saw profit opportunities elsewhere. Such investments grew substantially over the late 1970s and early 1980s, until the high real U.S. interest rates reversed the tide in 1983.[22] With the new institutional arrangements that facilitated such investment, these flows could grow again. Thus, some part of any increase in domestic saving is likely to flow overseas, increasing U.S. wealth but not the productivity of the U.S. work force.

In addition, increases in domestic saving do not necessarily flow to high-payoff business investments that will significantly increase economic growth. In fact, if the market system works, the investments that are already being made with the supply of capital actually available for investment are those with the greatest expected rate of return. If domestic investment increases, the additional investments will be those that would have failed the market test under the prior, smaller, supply of savings.[23] And if savings are devoted to investment in housing rather than to business capital, the productive capacity of the economy will not increase.

Finally, even the effect of increased productive investment is sometimes exaggerated. While a permanent increase in the investment share of GNP increases the level of output permanently, it increases the rate of growth of output only temporarily. Greater investment increases future output by increasing the size of the capital stock. The additional capital produces additional output as long as it is in operation, but eventually it wears out. Because depreciation on the larger capital stock is greater, it takes more investment

---

22. Council of Economic Advisers, *Economic Report of the President* (Washington, D.C.: U.S. Government Printing Office, February 1984), table B-99, p. 333.

23. Edward F. Denison, "The Unimportance of the Embodied Question," *American Economic Review*, vol. 54, March 1964, part 1, pp. 90-94.

just to replace the capital that wears out every year. Eventually, the capital stock reaches a size at which the additional depreciation is equal to the additional investment because of the higher investment share of GNP. At that time, growth reverts to its previous rate. So there is a temporary increase in the rate of economic growth as the economy climbs to a higher level of output, but growth gradually recedes to its long-term rate.[24]

Obviously, none of these many considerations is an argument against more saving and investment. All else being equal, the nation will always be at least as well off with a bigger capital stock. Nonetheless, taxation and capital formation must be viewed realistically. It is often implicitly assumed that (1) there is a potential for substantial increases in saving through changes in tax policy, and (2) such increases in saving would substantially increase investment and the rate of growth of the U.S. economy. On the basis of the empirical research and the analyses of the workings of our economic institutions cited here, both these propositions are probably wrong.

Taxation and Resource Allocation

Although there is little evidence that tax policy can significantly increase factor supply and economic growth, taxes can influence economic performance in other ways. Many tax law provisions influence taxpayer decisions relating to the allocation of resources. Preferential tax law provisions for production of oil or timber, or for investment in energy conservation or in research and development, among many others, can induce shifts of investment into the tax-preferred activities.

In general, these distortions of economic choices reduce the national income. In the absence of taxes, resources flow to the activities that yield the greatest social return—that is, the greatest profit. But a tax preference can make an activity with a lesser social return more profitable after taxes. It follows that national income falls when investment is so transferred.

Some tax preferences can be justified despite their ill effects on the allocation of resources. Markets do not consider noneconomic factors. For example, the political costs of the uncertainty of the Middle East oil supply could justify subsidies for energy conservation and domestic oil production. But counterarguments could be raised: the tax preferences enacted because of such nonmarket considerations must be efficient—they must accomplish their goals at low cost. Our oil production subsidies, for example, may not

---

24. Other factors such as returns to scale and the supply of labor affect the size of the increase of output and the speed of approach to the new level of output. Bosworth, *Tax Incentives and Economic Growth*, pp. 44-47.

in fact increase production, because nontax factors may be more important. Many other tax preferences are well intended but have significant technical flaws. Some tax preferences may accrue to taxpayers only because of their political influence; other preferences might have made sense at some time in the past but have outlived their usefulness.

Even some tax law provisions that are ostensibly general in their application can divert resources from their best uses. The Accelerated Cost Recovery System (ACRS), the cost recovery system for all depreciable physical investment, has widely documented misallocational effects.[25] The ACRS allowances are relatively more generous for investments in some equipment with particular useful lives; those investments are therefore more attractive to investors. Some forms of equipment are used more heavily in particular industries by the very nature of their production processes; industries that use primarily tax-favored equipment are themselves disproportionately benefited by the tax law. Similarly, the sharp reduction in depreciable lives for structures in ACRS diverts investment into certain types of buildings. The general investment tax credit may discriminate among different types of equipment. Even the tax preferences for individual taxpayers have distortionary effects; the tax subsidies for homeowners have long been alleged to divert investment into owner-occupied housing.

Several economists have attempted to measure the misallocations of resources because of ACRS. Assumptions and methodologies differ, but a moderate estimate of the effect of the distortion is an annual loss equivalent to almost $20 billion of output. Although this figure appears to be small, it would take a capital stock more than $200 billion larger to make up that loss permanently.[26] And this estimate includes only the misallocations attributable to ACRS; it does not include resources wasted because of other nonneutralities in the tax law. All these resource losses are quite hard to evaluate, of course; if tax-induced distortions take resources away from industries in which international competition is keen and prospects for growth are great, the cost to the United States in the long run could be considerable.

Conclusions on Efficiency

So despite all the recent emphasis on using tax policy to increase the supply of labor and capital and thus the rate of economic growth, there is

---

25. For example, Hulten and Robertson, "Corporate Tax Policy and Economic Growth."

26. Jane G. Gravelle, "Capital Income Taxation and Efficiency in the Allocation of Investment," *National Tax Journal*, vol. 36, September 1983, pp. 297-306. The figure cited includes the misallocations of capital among business and consumer durables and land.

little promise of success. The entire area is clouded by uncertainties in the theoretical, statistical, and institutional relationships among the influences on, and the indicators of, economic performance. Despite the undeniable appeal in principle of greater capital formation as a stimulant to growth, there is little evidence that it is possible to increase capital formation through tax policy, or even that such a policy, if successful, would have a significant long-term effect on growth. It is still too early to pass judgment on the 1981 tax cuts, which could be an indicator of the prospects of such policies, but it is clear that the rewards of those tax cuts, if any, have not yet materialized.

There are demonstrable but more subtle costs to our current tax system that policy could reduce. The tax law causes economic distortions that a more neutral law could minimize. Tax neutrality would lead to allocation of resources to their most profitable uses, and thus would yield greater economic efficiency and incomes. The effect on the economy would not be large, but neither would it be inconsequential.

With budgetary considerations paramount, it may make sense for tax policy to focus on neutrality. Increasing tax revenues requires either eliminating some tax preferences—which makes the tax system more neutral—or raising tax rates. Raising the tax rates would magnify existing nonneutralities in the tax law and blunt incentives as well. But a deficit reduction policy that eliminated or cut back tax preferences, perhaps far enough to justify lower tax rates, could increase tax revenues and neutrality.

A strategy focused heavily on capital formation could impose tax rates on income from capital that are lower than tax rates on income from labor. Indeed, as chapter 5 explains, the widely discussed personal expenditure tax allows an effective tax exemption for income from capital. Such a system may win high marks from some analysts, but others would challenge its merits on efficiency and other grounds.

So, efficiency in taxation, like fairness, proves to be an elusive commodity. It cannot be obtained in infinite supply, and what we get comes at a price. And yet the current tax law is so inefficient in its pursuit of efficiency that we might hope to get more efficiency at little additional cost, if tax policy is carefully made.

CHAPTER 4

MAKING THE TAX SYSTEM SIMPLER

The federal income tax is roundly criticized as too complex. In 1983, 41 percent of all taxpayers had their returns filled out by professional tax preparers. But in that same year, 38 percent of all taxpayers filed on one of the two short forms (1040A and 1040 EZ); another 26 percent claimed the standard deduction (or zero bracket amount) on the regular form 1040.[1]

How can these seemingly contradictory facts be reconciled?

What Is Tax Simplicity?

A superficial definition of tax simplicity is easy to formulate: a tax should be easy for taxpayers to understand and for tax administrators to collect.

Unfortunately, we cannot completely achieve this theoretical goal in practice. Simplicity for one group of taxpayers may come only at the price of complexity for others; and pursuit of simplicity in some respects can clash with goals of increasing fairness and economic efficiency. In the final analysis, tax simplicity must be traded off against other values, and different kinds of simplicity must be weighed against each other in setting our goals.

But even beyond these policy considerations, there remains something of a puzzle. Despite undeniable overall complexity, the federal income tax for the average taxpayer (who claims the standard deduction or modest amounts of itemized deductions) is not all that complicated. Moreover, the IRS will even compute the taxes of people who have relatively simple economic affairs (and who might otherwise be the most intimidated by the overall tax system). Is complexity really near the top of the list of public concerns about the

---

1. Dorothea Riley, ''Individual Income Tax Returns: Selected Characteristics from the 1983 Taxpayer Usage Study,'' U.S. Department of the Treasury, Internal Revenue Service, *Statistics of Income Bulletin*, Summer 1984, pp. 45-64.

income tax? If so, could complexity really be just a proxy for something else,
a stand-in for some other problems that taxpayers believe complexity causes?
Can we ever achieve a system that typical taxpayers will accept as simple,
or will they always sense complexity even if the system for most filers is
kept quite simple? If taxpayers are to respect the income tax, these questions
may be as important as questions about complexity itself.

Simplicity for Whom?

The tax system affects different kinds of taxpayers in different ways.
The burdens of compliance are greater for some than for others. In some
cases, a significant share of the recordkeeping and computation needed for
tax filing would have to be done even without an income tax.

Businesses

For many businesses, for example, tax simplification in the sense of
shorter and fewer tax forms is not a high priority. The number of forms to
be filled out, and the complexity of the forms, is hardly imposing for a General
Motors.

Furthermore, much of business tax accounting would need to be done
even without an income tax. Holders of stocks and bonds need to know cash
receipts, current expenses, debt service, and depreciation in order to evaluate
their investments. Accordingly, corporations are required to report such information.

Some complication arises because of differences between financial and
tax accounting. For example, tax depreciation and accounting depreciation
differ, and so firms must compute depreciation twice (or three times, if state
income tax depreciation is different from the other two). Of course, few firms
complain about this complication, because tax depreciation is more generous
than accounting depreciation; that is, tax depreciation allows the deduction
of capital costs sooner. If there were to be any greater conformity between
tax and accounting depreciation, business owners would probably prefer that
accounting depreciation be changed. (But it is not certain that businesses
would want a change. The current system may give businesses the best of
both worlds: attractive balance sheets, because slow accounting depreciation
reduces reported costs; and low taxes, because fast tax depreciation reduces
taxable income).

Is tax complexity therefore irrelevant for business? Not entirely. For one
thing, there is probably a differential burden of complexity on small as opposed
to large businesses. A large corporation can absorb the overhead to hire

personnel specialized in tax compliance, and once these people learn how to handle a particular type of transaction, they simply repeat that procedure again and again. The owner of a small proprietorship, on the other hand, might need to know much of what the entire tax staff of a large corporation collectively knows about taxation. And the proprietor's investment in time and effort to learn about tax depreciation, for example, might be used for only one transaction, whereas the large corporation can spread its investment in tax expertise over many transactions. In theory a small business can hire a tax preparer, but such a decision raises a second issue.

In the preceding chapter we noted that the income tax, with its special preferences and other nonneutralities, has come to influence economic decisions. For example, the tax law allows depreciation deduction schedules that favor some investments over others, and there is an investment credit for equipment but not for structures. These differences greatly complicate decision making by businesses: Should a firm replace a factory? Or should it merely replace the machines in the existing plant? Should it buy more durable or less durable machines? Should it expand into one or another line of business? These questions cannot be answered without careful reference to the tax law, and the answers in light of the tax considerations will sometimes differ from those based only on market forces.

It follows that compliance with a complex tax code is not easily separable from other business functions. If the income tax is a major factor in making business decisions, business owners must understand the tax law to make the right decisions. So the income tax can touch every facet of the operations of a large and complex firm, greatly complicating its planning. In addition, small businesses' proprietors cannot merely farm out their taxes; they must either learn every relevant nuance of the tax law themselves, or buy ongoing tax advice that encompasses many of their operating decisions as well as the completion of their tax forms.

So tax simplicity for businesses is not so much an issue of forms and computations as it is a question of the complexity of "making deals" under the influence of an intrusive tax law. In comparison with choosing the best investment in light of the special provisions in the tax code, filling out a business tax return is quite simple. If the tax law could be revised to intrude less on decision making, filling out business tax forms would hardly be a concern.

Individuals

As in the case of business taxation, simplicity in individual income taxation is desired by all but understood by few. For example, an advantage claimed for some tax reforms has been a tax return that fits on a postcard. Such a prospect is totally unrealistic. The space on the current return for the taxpayer's name, address, Social Security number, occupation, selection of type of return, names of dependents, reporting of amounts of income received and taxes withheld, and signature already exceeds the area of a large (five-inch by eight-inch) postcard. We simply cannot reduce this basic minimum amount of information on the tax return. Another issue is the graduated rate schedule; flat-rate tax schemes are billed as significant simplifications, because taxpayers will not have to use tax tables.[2] But the IRS supplies tax tables as a simplification, to reduce the number of computations needed; experience shows that reducing the number of computations reduces the number of errors. If tax tables were used with a flat-rate tax, as they certainly would be, taxpayers would see no difference at all from the current graduated rate system. So just what is simplicity in the individual income tax?

As was noted earlier, most taxpayers do not itemize deductions, and more than a third use one of the two shortened forms. For those taxpayers, the tax-filing process is far from complex. In fact, taxpayers with incomes under $50,000 mostly in wages and salaries and no itemized deductions can send in their W-2 forms (the forms employers give to their employeee reporting their total wage income) and have the Internal Revenue Service figure the tax due. Taxes cannot get much simpler than that.

And yet more than 40 percent of all returns in 1983 were signed by paid tax preparers—including 18 percent of those filing on the short forms. Why are so many taxpayers with simple returns going to professional preparers?

There may be many reasons to hire someone to fill out a tax return; complexity is just one of them. There certainly are people who can manage to earn a living but who cannot fill out even the short form; thus, there probably will always be a core of taxpayers with relatively simple economic affairs who will need professional help to comply with the system. But no matter how simple or complex the tax forms may be, completing a tax return is certainly tedious. One wouldn't imagine a national revolt over the complexity of lawnmowers because millions of homeowners hire professionals to cut their grass; perhaps we should not be shocked by a tendency of taxpayers to hire tax preparers.

Some taxpayers have complex financial transactions. Owners of small businesses may need a professional accountant to keep their books, and that accountant would probably fill out the tax return. Other taxpayers have com-

---

2. A flat-rate tax would simplify such taxpayer decisions as allocations of income between spouses or among taxable years, but these are not major sources of complication for the income tax.

plex investments, or even a one-time sale of stock or a home that they would rather have handled professionally.

Other reasons for paying a tax preparer may be somewhat disturbing from the point of view of tax administration. One might be a fear of the consequences of making a mistake—having to pay interest and a penalty and possibly even having an innocent mistake misinterpreted as fraud. More relevant to policy is taxpayer fear of missing out on some special feature or "loophole" in the tax system, and thereby paying more than is really due. This fear may well be caused, at least in part, by the complexity of the tax forms and instructions.

Complexity and Taxpayer Attitudes. Although typical taxpayers complain to pollsters that the tax forms and instructions are too complex, the basic tax provisions for those in ordinary circumstances are really fairly simple. When the many special incentives and subsidies are considered, however, the tax law appears extraordinarily complex. And although the bulk of the law may be irrelevant to typical taxpayers, they must confront the whole code when they seek to fill out their returns. This mass of detail may well suggest that other taxpayers can use the minutiae to pay less—thereby breeding widespread resentment. And some recent provisions designed to promote fairness seem instead to impose complexity on typical taxpayers.

In 1983, the Form 1040 instruction booklet amounted to forty-six closely packed pages, not counting the forms themselves. The complete information booklet underlying the 1040 package, titled *Your Income Tax*, was 176 pages long. There were at least seventy-six forms pertinent to the individual income tax, although some were infrequently used. The free market obviously sees an opportunity in all this paper; several large commercially available income tax guides are aimed at ordinary taxpayers filing their own returns.

The Form 1040 instruction booklet is the main form of communication between the individual taxpayer and the tax system, and therefore deserves a closer look. Eighteen of the forty-six pages pertain to basic questions for taxpayers who could file the short form (Form 1040A). Chief among the questions answered for these taxpayers are how to choose the proper type of return to file (from among joint, surviving spouse, married filing separately, head of household, and single returns) and whether another person qualifies as a dependent. These questions are likely to persist under any realistic tax reform. Another three pages pertain only to itemized deductions, and thus are relevant for only the one-third of taxpayers who itemize. So long as mortgage interest, state and local taxes, and charitable contributions remain deductible, most of this material will remain in the book.

Thus, it is unlikely that the tax forms and instructions facing the typical taxpayer can be significantly simplified; they really are not all that complicated now. Beyond the short form, even the common itemized deductions are quite simple. The amounts of the mortgage interest and property tax deductions are reported to homeowners by their lenders at the end of the year. Deductible state and local income tax withholdings are reported by employers. Charitable contributions must be totaled by the taxpayer, but typically do not involve a large number of transactions; many taxpayers' major contributions are to United Way campaigns through payroll deduction and thus are reported by employers. So the heart of the ordinary tax return is really quite straightforward, and much of the computation and paperwork are really done by employers and mortgage lenders.

The IRS has tried to simplify further through providing shorter forms for those in basic tax circumstances. Thus, the Form 1040A is available to taxpayers with mostly wage income who do not itemize. The new form 1040EZ is even simpler for some single taxpayers (eliminating the need for instructions relating to dependents). These forms do in fact make life easier for the people who can use them, but there is an important limit to their effectiveness. If taxpayers are concerned that they are missing out on legal provisions that could reduce their taxes, a shorter form and instructions may only heighten the fear of being left out. The IRS might be seen as actively concealing such loopholes by distributing shorter forms and instruction booklets that don't include them. Cautionary notes on the short forms advising certain taxpayers to investigate the longer forms might be too complex and jargon-filled for some taxpayers to understand. Thus, the IRS could be in a no-win situation: if the tax forms are too long, they are seen as complex; but if the forms are too short, they may not include all of the information a taxpayer needs to pay the least permissible tax.

Recent experience suggests that resentment at missing out on tax loopholes has some basis in fact. In the 1981 tax law, the Congress enacted a special tax deduction for two-earner married couples. When the 1982 tax returns (the first to which the deduction applied) were filed, the IRS reported that many eligible couples did not claim the deduction.[3] Because the deduction was "free money" to those couples—they reported and paid tax on the earned income that made them eligible—there was no reason for them not to claim the deduction other than ignorance of its existence or confusion at its complexity. Any ignorance surely is caused by a resistance to wading through the lengthy instructions, and an underlying distaste for the complexity of the system. Research on the equally complex income averaging provision, and eligible taxpayers' failure to use it, leads to the same conclusion.[4]

---

3. Department of the Treasury, Internal Revenue Service press release, March 17, 1983.

4. Eugene Steuerle, Richard McHugh and Emil M. Sunley, "Who Benefits from Income Averaging?" *National Tax Journal*, vol. 31, March 1978, pp. 19-32.

If an eligible couple does not claim the special two-earner deduction, the IRS can remedy the situation; most of the information needed to determine if a couple is eligible is reported on the regular form. This is also generally true of the exceedingly complicated refundable earned-income credit, which is designed to provide relief from income and payroll taxes for low-income working families with children. (This is not the case if such a family has an income so low that it is not legally required to file and chooses not to file, perhaps in ignorance of the credit's existence.) Checking returns for such missing preferences slows the system, however, and taxpayers reap their savings only after a long delay. And although taxpayers might be reassured if the IRS reminds them of a preference they did not claim, they might also be made suspicious about what *other* benefits they are missing.

There are many other tax provisions that do not provide a built-in check on the standard tax forms. For example, the same 1981 tax legislation introduced a deduction for charitable contributions by nonitemizers; they may claim this special deduction in addition to the standard deduction. In 1982, 65 percent of all nonitemizers did not claim the special deduction, and 60 percent did not claim it in 1983;[5] it is unlikely that all those nonitemizers made no charitable contributions at all. All itemized deductions fall into the same category; if an itemizer forgets to claim a deduction or is unaware that the deduction is available, there is no way the IRS can rectify the error.

As the tax code accumulates new features like the two-earner deduction, the earned-income credit, and the extra deduction for charitable contributions, even the short form has become longer. Now that these complex provisions are aimed at even the lowest-income taxpayers and as errors and omissions with respect to these tax features multiply,[6] we can expect taxpayers' suspicions and resentments to become even worse. Trying to equalize the tax system with "loopholes for the masses" may be a costly strategy in terms of complexity.

And if the most common and general tax preferences confuse ordinary taxpayers, the more exotic features of the law must cause even more difficulty. The Form 1040 instruction booklet does not deal with the special features such as oil depletion and expensing of intangible drilling costs, capital gains treatment of certain forms of income, and others. These special provisions

---

5. Dorothea Riley, "Individual Income Tax Returns: Selected Characteristics From the 1982 Taxpayer Usage Study," U.S. Department of the Treasury, Internal Revenue Service, vol. 3, Summer 1983, pp. 43-56; and idem, "Individual Income Tax Returns: Selected Characteristics From the 1983 Taxpayer Usage Study," vol. 4, Summer, 1984, pp. 45-62.

6. For example, in 1982, 5 percent of all taxpayers using the charitable contributions deduction for nonitemizers claimed more than the legal maximum $25 deduction. This error persisted in 1983. Riley, "Individual Income Tax Returns."

probably cause the public to tell pollsters that the wealthy pay little or no tax. Although the public's estimate of the frequency and success of large-scale tax avoidance is exaggerated, there are constant reminders of such strategies in public advertisements for tax shelters. As long as tax sheltering remains before the public eye, many taxpayers with no access to such means of tax avoidance will feel cheated. This sentiment is a driving force for basic tax reform.

So why do so many people hire professional tax preparers to fill out the short form? Not because the short form itself is too complicated, but because the totality of the tax law is too complicated. If only a tax professional can know and understand all or even most of the loopholes in the law, then typical taxpayers must see a professional to be sure that they do not miss out on something. Tax experts may chuckle knowingly that most typical taxpayers have no complex loopholes and so waste their money on paid preparers, but the taxpayers cannot know this without the professional advice.

As long as the tax law remains arcane and continues to conceal lucrative nooks and crannies—and this means both tax loopholes *and* high marginal rates of tax—taxpayers will continue to see tax preparers. Repeal of those special features simplifies the law not just for those taxpayers who use them but for *all* taxpayers—saving some the time and expense of wading through the extra instructions and forms or of hiring professional help to learn that they are *not* eligible to use them.

But we should be realistic in our expectations of even a fully streamlined tax law. The tax-preparer industry may be cut back, but it will never disappear.

A further question is whether the bulk of taxpayers can ever be convinced that there is no need to comb the tax law, either alone or with professional help, in search of tax loopholes. If only specialists can understand the tax law now, how will nonspecialists know if the law is meaningfully simplified? The answer may lie in the treatment of tax questions in the popular press—both in the reporting of tax manipulation practices and trends and in the advertising of tax shelter deals. Such secondhand information may have exaggerated the *extent* of successful tax avoidance in the past, but it will surely communicate the *direction of change* in the future. If tax professionals find that opportunities for manipulation and sheltering are reduced, word will get around.

A final question is whether typical taxpayers will see a substantial simplification of their own tax returns; here, the answer is no. As was explained earlier, the current short form 1040A, and even the standard form 1040, are not all that complex. Even an ambitious restructuring of the tax code would remove only a few lines and pages of instructions from the typical taxpayer's return. Nonetheless, the elimination of even obscure provisions would reduce the need for most people to search for sources of advantage—and this, in turn, will relieve them of a burden of time and expense.

Tax Administrators

Complexity bedevils the tax system as well as the taxpayers. Masses of longer and more complex tax returns take more time to process. That same complexity drains IRS resources from the audit and examination functions that maintain compliance and public respect for the tax system and the government. With the number of individual income tax returns now approaching 100 million per year, and with almost 3 million additional corporate and estate tax returns, control of the administrative load is essential.

Unlike individual taxpayers, tax administrators are hardly fazed by mathematical computation. Tax returns are checked by computer, and so marginal changes in the computational load are not the most serious burden, even with the large number of tax returns. What is burdensome is checking the validity of the numbers reported and claimed on the return, not the accuracy with which they are added together.

Here again, complexity arises from the proliferation of special provisions and tax subsidies in the code. Many of the special provisions are designed to encourage particular kinds of activity and to cushion particular kinds of hardship, and they have little bearing on the central purpose of raising revenue. Examples are the investment tax credit, designed to encourage investment in machinery; and the medical expense deduction, intended to cushion the financial blow of illness.

Such tax subsidies are sometimes justified as simpler and cheaper to administer than the alternative of direct spending programs for the same purposes. The arguments are (1) that the tax forms need to be filled out anyway, and so a few additional lines or pages of instructions will not make much difference; and that (2) money is changing hands between the taxpayer and the government anyway, making the financial transaction easier.

These arguments are valid in some cases, but direct subsidies and tax subsidies, as now administered, are not comparable programs. For one thing, tax subsidies can give benefits or rewards that bear little relationship to the ostensible purposes of the programs. For example, a profitable firm can reduce its taxes through the investment tax credit, but new and unprofitable firms, with no tax liability, get no current benefit. Similarly, top-bracket taxpayers can save 50 cents on each deductible dollar of medical expenses, whereas bottom-bracket taxpayers save only 11 cents, and taxpayers who claim the standard deduction or who are not taxable save nothing at all. Direct spending programs through government matching grants could distribute the benefits in a more rational way.

A second difference between tax and spending programs is that tax programs are subject to far less exacting verification.[7] Just over 1 percent of all individual income tax returns are audited. In contrast, most generally comparable federal spending programs are much more carefully scrutinized, with the government frequently examining documentation or inspecting to verify that requirements are met. Thus, the supposed efficiency advantages of tax subsidies are due largely to a lesser degree of verification.

In addition, to the extent that tax subsidies are verified, tax personnel who are not expert in investment, or medical care, or some other field, must judge whether the claims of subsidies are justified. The IRS cannot fulfill such specialized roles as well as the pertinent agencies, and any such specialized verification must slow processing of the tax return. As examples of these problems, disputes over the distinction between machinery eligible for the investment tax credit, on the one hand, and structures ineligible, on the other, forced the Congress to legislate a categorization of chicken coops.[8] Similarly, the tax courts had to resolve a taxpayer's claim of a medical expense deduction for the construction of an indoor swimming pool in his home for purposes of medically prescribed exercise.[9] These are just extreme cases of constant problems regarding the classification of investment assets, of medically prescribed vacations, home improvements, cosmetic surgery, and matters relevant to other parts of the code. The burden of these decisions extends well beyond what tax administrators should be expected to do.

Thus, simplifying the tax system for tax administrators is a worthwhile task because in many ways it simplifies the system for everyone. Faster processing of returns and greater compliance are in everyone's interest. As with businesses and individuals, simplicity requires that the tax system focus on raising revenue and avoid complicated provisions with other goals. Many questions that confuse and preoccupy taxpayers are also troublesome for tax administrators.

---

7. Jerome Kurtz, "A Broad-Base Tax—An Idea Whose Time Has Come," *The New Tax Reform of the '80s: A Broad-Base System?* (Dallas, Texas: The LTV Corporation, 1982), pp. 15-24, is central to much of the following discussion.

8. "Investment Credit for Single Purpose Agricultural Structures," Section 314 of the Revenue Act of 1978, P.L. 95-600.

9. "Taking the Plunge: How One Taxpayer Justified a Swimming Pool Deduction," *Wall Street Journal*, August 31, 1983, p.1.

Interactions

Earlier chapters discussed the pursuit of fairness and economic efficiency through tax policy. In fact, those pursuits often add to the complexity of the tax law for taxpayer and tax administrator alike.

Such complexity arises through attempted "fine tuning" of tax preferences for fairness or efficiency. For example, restrictions on deductions and credits are required to limit the tax benefits to particular taxpayers or types of expenses. As a result, the law and forms can be complicated beyond any compensating gain in fairness or efficiency. Two examples will illustrate this trade-off among tax goals.

Medical Expenses. The deduction for medical expenses was enacted in 1942.[10] The rationale for the deduction is that medical care costs are involuntary expenses required to maintain health, and so taxpayers burdened with such costs have a lesser ability to pay tax than others with the same income but no such expenses. The deduction has always been restricted to medical expenses in excess of some percentage of adjusted gross income. The rationale for this restriction is that every taxpayer has some medical expenses, just as every taxpayer must buy some food to sustain life; the point of the deduction was to compensate for only extraordinary medical expenses, and the income percentage floor was to prevent deduction of normal health care costs.

In 1954, however, the Congress sought to rectify what it saw as a flaw in the deduction.[11] Taxpayers were seen as claiming excessive deductions for the costs of medicines and drugs, including nonprescription medicines. The belief was that such costs bore their own normal relationship to income, and that they should be tested separately to determine if they were in fact extraordinary. As a result, a second income test was added to the deduction: only medicine and drug costs in excess of 1 percent of adjusted gross income were added to doctor and hospital expenses, and the excess of that total over 3 percent of adjusted gross income was deductible.

Then in 1965, the Congress added an incentive feature to the deduction.[12] Medical insurance costs had been deductible in the same fashion as doctor or hospital bills. The Congress, however, wanted a positive inducement to buy insurance; it feared that people would unwisely refuse insurance, knowing that the cost probably would not be deductible (because it would not exceed

---

10. U.S. Senate, Committee on the Budget, *Tax Expenditures: Relationship to Spending Programs and Background Material on Individual Provisions* (Washington, D.C.: U.S. Government Printing Office, March 17, 1982), pp. 238–39.

11. Ibid.

12. Ibid.

3 percent of income), and instead would bank on the tax deduction for any expenses that would arise. So the Congress allowed a deduction for one-half of all medical insurance premiums (but no more than $150) irrespective of other spending on health care and of income. The balance of medical insurance premiums was added to hospital and doctor bills and could be deducted if that spending exceeded the 3 percent of income test. After this change, the deduction remained largely unaltered until 1982.

Each of these policy steps had some rationale with respect to fairness (and at the time, the incentive for purchasing health insurance might have been billed as a move toward efficiency as well). Piled on top of one another, however, these conditions made the deduction an exercise in mathematical and logical gymnastics. Taxpayers first had to calculate the lesser of one-half of their health insurance premiums or $150; that amount was put aside to be deducted from taxable income regardless of the outcome of the further calculations. Then the taxpayers summed their expenses on medicines and drugs and found the excess of that amount over 1 percent of their adjusted gross income. That amount was added to the balance of their health insurance premiums and all their doctor and hospital bills, and the sum was compared with 3 percent of adjusted gross income. This balance was then added to the deductible medical insurance premiums computed earlier to arrive at the final deduction. These maneuvers proved so complex that in its detailed study of 1979, the IRS found that 58.3 percent of all claimants of the medical expense deduction made some mistake. And this was not all overstating of deductions; 25.8 percent of those taxpayers understated their deductions.[13]

The medical expense deduction was simplified in the Tax Equity and Fiscal Responsibility Act of 1982 (TEFRA); the separate deduction for medical insurance and the separate treatment of medicines and drugs were eliminated (only prescription drug costs are now deductible), and the income threshold for total medical expenses was increased to 5 percent of adjusted gross income. These changes eliminated some of the fine-tuning of fairness and some of the extraordinary complexity of the deduction. (The changes also reduced some taxpayers' deductions to zero.) Nonetheless, the history of the medical expense deduction remains a case study of how concern with fairness or efficiency can leave the tax law unmanageably complex. Whatever the primary goals of tax proposals, they must be weighed against any resulting complication.

---

13. U.S. Department of the Treasury, Internal Revenue Service, Taxpayer Compliance Monitoring Program data, processed.

Capital Gains. Capital gains have received special treatment under the income tax since 1922. Although the precise terms have changed many times, some portion of capital gains on assets held for some minimum period of time has been excluded from tax since that year.

There are three major reasons for the capital gains preference. First, the exclusion of some portion of capital gains from tax allegedly encourages investors to undertake the risky investments that yield capital gains. Without such a preference, it is argued, too much saving would flow toward safe investments. Second, the exclusion is said to compensate for inflation. The entire dollar amount of an asset's appreciation is considered to be a capital gain for tax purposes, even though some of that appreciation merely compensates the owner for the depreciation, by subsequent inflation, of the principal that was originally invested. (At the same time, however, capital gains are taxed only when realized. Thus, owners of assets can postpone the tax indefinitely, and can realize the gain and pay the tax at a time of their own choosing. Furthermore, income tax on the capital gain is implicitly forgiven if the owner dies before realizing the gain. These advantages could offset or even outweigh the disadvantage of paying tax on nominal gains.) Third, a large capital gain is in effect "bunched" in one year, and therefore taxed at higher marginal rates than would be the case if the gain were spread over all the years the asset was held.

The complicating factor in the capital gains preference, as in virtually every other preference, is that everyone wants to get under the preferential umbrella. With the capital gains preference quite large—under the current law, tax on a capital gain is only 40 percent of the tax on a comparable amount of ordinary income (that is, income other than that from capital gains)—there is a lot of money at stake. Various devices have been developed to transform ordinary income into capital gain, and the tax law has had to be changed as a result. Numerous legal provisions were added to define various forms of income into or out of the capital gains category. As one tax law expert put it, "The subject singly responsible for the largest amount of complexity is the treatment of capital gains and losses."[14]

The preference for long-term capital gains contributes to an awkward situation for long-term capital losses. The offsetting of capital losses against ordinary income must be restricted. Without some restriction, taxpayers with large, diversified portfolios could realize their losses but hold their gains, use

---

14. Stanley S. Surrey, "Definitional Problems in Capital Gains Taxation," *Tax Revision Compendium*, Papers Submitted to House Committee on Ways and Means (1959), vol. 2, p. 1203.

the losses to offset all of their ordinary income, and pay no tax. With an exclusion of part of long-term capital gains, however, there must be a further exclusion for part of long-term capital losses, to prevent taxpayers from realizing identical long-term gains and losses and winding up with excess losses to offset other income.

The capital gains exclusion is a major ingredient of tax shelters. Tax shelter investments are designed to provide early tax deductions (such as interest and depreciation), and to yield their net income in the form of long-term capital gains. Taxes are deferred, and the eventual tax liability is reduced by the capital gains exclusion. Enormous shares of IRS enforcement and tax court resources must be spent policing tax shelter activity. The number of pending shelter cases before the tax court has increased to more than 20,000.[15]

One relatively new form of tax shelter is the straddle, which plays directly on the distinction between long- and short-term gains. The basic straddle involves both buying and selling (that is, selling short) the same or a nearly equivalent security at the same time. The taxpayer liquidates the losing position before the minimum holding period, so that the loss can be deducted in full; the gain is realized after the minimum holding period, so that only 40 percent of the gain is subject to tax. Obviously, tax straddles contribute nothing to the economy because there is no net investment. The 1981 tax law attempted to deal with straddles, unsuccessfully, and the 1984 tax law had to make a second try to finish the job.

The capital gains exclusion probably does affect investment. Although there is no measurable effect of capital gains tax cuts on total investment (not surprising, because so much of the funds that are invested come from nontaxable entities such as pension funds), there may be some leverage on particular kinds of investments, such as venture capital. Nonetheless, as in the case of the medical care deduction, a nontax objective can be pursued only at the cost of considerable complexity, both for taxpayers and administrators. In this case, the complexity helped to create an entire tax shelter industry whose product is pure tax avoidance that distorts economic decisions and reduces output.

No Return Taxes

The Internal Revenue Service has been working on a "return-free" system, under which the IRS could compute taxes without any tax return

15. "ABA Tax Section Rails Against Tax Shelters," *Tax Notes*, vol. 23, June 4, 1984, pp. 1018-19.

being filed.[16] The "return-free" system would allow those taxpayers who are already eligible to have the IRS compute their liability to file no return at all if they so arrange in advance with the IRS. This approach would simplify April 15 for some taxpayers, but it would have its limitations.

For one thing, the IRS obviously would need all the information now on the tax return to figure the tax due. Thus, the taxpayer would have to provide all that information at some time; the difference would be that the taxpayer could provide the information earlier in the year, not all at the last minute and not in the potentially confrontational atmosphere of a tax return. Some information (such as a W-2 form, showing wage or salary income and withholding) might be sent to the IRS directly by an employer or bank without a separate and additional submission by the taxpayer.

A second limitation is that the taxpayer's economic circumstances must be simple—about as simple as those now required for the short forms. If a taxpayer has several sources of unpredictable amounts of income, the IRS workload—particularly at the end of the tax year, when liabilities must be completed—would be excessive. Similarly, the IRS could not process information documents for numerous individual medical expenses and charitable contributions. Right now, the IRS processes information documents on the receipt of income items (mostly interest and dividends) and some itemized deductions (mortgage interest and some state and local taxes) on a sampling basis, for purposes of spot-checking compliance. Gathering *all* information documents for income, more besides for deductions, and then computing complete tax liabilities for a significant share of the population would be an administrative task several orders of magnitude removed from the current situation.

Thus, the prospective IRS "return-free" system could apply only to taxpayers claiming the standard deduction, and even then only to those using a minimum of other special features of the tax law. The Treasury Department has estimated that the system could be used by about half of all taxpayers—certainly those with the simplest returns. For many of those taxpayers, a "return-free" system would be a noticeable relief from the compliance burden. In today's system with its many special provisions, however, using the "return-free" approach might require forgoing opportunities to claim deductions or credits and thereby reduce one's taxes; this feature unquestionably would make the system less attractive (unless many of those special provisions were repealed).

---

16. U.S. Department of the Treasury, *Tax Reform for Fairness, Simplicity, and Economic Growth: The Treasury Department Report to the President*, (Washington, D.C.: U.S. Government Printing Office, November 1984), vol. 1, p. xi.

Conclusion

There is considerable potential for simplification of the income tax, but it is not a simplification that typical taxpayers would see in the course of filling out their returns. What they could well sense—and might also see as a significant benefit—is the absence of complex legal provisions which they could not use, or could use only with professional help, but which other people have been routinely using to cut their taxes. Thus, complexity may be seen not as a problem in its own right but as a problem because of the unfairness it is perceived to create.

Recent experience suggests that many taxpayers have considerable difficulty using beneficial provisions in the current law, such as the deduction for two-earner couples and income averaging. If ordinary taxpayers cannot cope with such provisions intended for general use, it is no wonder that they consider the rest of the law arcane.

No realistic tax restructuring could drastically simplify the short form; the most one could hope for is removal of a few lines. The really fine print of the tax code is not on the short form and does not apply to most American families. But if clearing out that fine print would convince most Americans that they can use the short form without paying extra tax and would allow businesses to base their decisions on the marketplace instead of the tax code, the effort would be worthwhile.

CHAPTER 5

MAKING THE SHORT LIST: TAXING CONSUMPTION

The federal tax structure needs basic reform, and the federal treasury needs more revenue. Fundamental tax restructuring would be an important step forward for public policy and may be a prerequisite for revenue action to narrow the deficit.

Despite the failings of the current system and despite the need for more revenue-raising capacity, action requires an alternative. There is no shortage of candidates, but they all fall into two basic categories: (1) taxes on consumption; and (2) taxes on income. Both types have advantages and disadvantages. The choice will come from the weighing of those pluses and minuses, not from the obvious dominance of one over the other.

This chapter analyzes the options that involve taxing consumption. The following chapter discusses the income tax options.

Taxing Consumption: the Rationale

Recently, some policymakers and economists have expressed much interest in taxing consumption rather than income. Some of this interest comes from philosophical value judgments. As Thomas Hobbes argued, consumption is what people take out of society's accumulation of wealth, but income is the measure of what they put in; thus, income is to be rewarded and consumption discouraged by taxation, rather than the other way around.[1] Taxing consumption, therefore, has the connotation of favoring foresight and thrift. This argument has been challenged on the same philosophical grounds; it is hard to argue on principle for the moral primacy of saving over consumption when the ultimate purpose of saving is later consumption.

---

1. Thomas Hobbes, *The Leviathan* (New York: Collier Books, 1962), Chapter 30, pp. 254-55.

This argument is pertinent to our recent economic sluggishness, which many economists attribute to our low national rate of saving and the consequent aging and obsolescence of our capital stock. The United States saved only 17.3 percent of its gross domestic product in the latter half of the 1970s; in contrast, Japan saved 29.3 percent and West Germany 21.0 percent.[2] Some economists argue that productivity in the United States would be higher, and long-run economic growth faster, if we as an economy saved more.

An income tax on both wages and interest taxes income when it is earned; the interest on any savings from that income is then taxed again. Some tax experts call this a double tax on savings. In contrast, consumption taxes in effect exempt capital income from taxation. (If the income tax were replaced by a tax on consumption, income from capital would not bear tax until it was consumed. As is explained later in this chapter, that postponement of tax is equivalent to a tax exemption.) If we taxed consumption, it is argued, people would choose to consume less and therefore would save more. If that saving were then devoted to domestic business capital formation, our capital stock, productivity, and future standard of living would be greater.

Behind the logic of this argument lies considerable uncertainty; it is not clear that such a policy change in the real world would live up to its billing. There is no theoretical reason why eliminating the income tax on saving should increase saving, as was noted in chapter 3. On the one hand, it would raise the after-tax rate of return, making saving more attractive; but on the other, it would reduce the amount of savings needed to attain any given target level of future wealth, making less saving necessary. Thus, the theoretical effect on saving of shifting from an income tax to a consumption tax is ambiguous. Actual taxpayer behavior since World War II has shown no evidence of a strong response to tax policy changes, even from the large 1981 tax cuts. And if we take into account the further questions regarding the payoff of any additional saving and investment we can induce, as enumerated in chapter 3, the economic growth case for consumption taxation is less than ironclad.

A complementary limit on the benefits of consumption taxation is its treatment of income from labor. Eliminating the taxation of income from capital may give greater incentives to save, but incentive questions also arise with respect to the supply of labor. If taxes on capital are eliminated in a revenue-short world, the entire yield of the abolished tax on capital income must be loaded onto labor. Although the responsiveness of labor supply to

---

2. Barry P. Bosworth, *Tax Incentives and Economic Growth* (Washington, D.C.: The Brookings Institution, 1974), table 3-2, p. 92.

tax rates is also controversial, there is little evidence that saving is sufficiently more sensitive to justify a wholesale shift of the tax burden from capital to labor.[3]

Thus, no form of consumption tax, as either a replacement for or a supplement to our tax system, is an easy path to faster economic growth. Some economists support such a tax for other reasons. Some, recognizing the limitations, want a marginal increase in saving for the benefits that it would yield. Nonetheless, we should have no illusions of a quantum leap in our economic well-being from a shift to taxing consumption.

Within the class of expenditure taxes, there are two distinct subgroups: taxes collected by businesses on individual transactions, and taxes collected from households on an annual basis. Each of these is discussed in the paragraphs that follow.

Taxes on Transactions

Taxing transactions is the simplest way to tax consumption; it would not require tax returns from households. Nonetheless, administering a transactions tax probably would be more complicated than many people would think—especially in its inevitable interaction with the income tax. Much complexity arises when we use the income tax to undo one of the basic but undesirable effects of a tax on retail sales: the burden on low-income households.

There are two basic kinds of expenditure taxes on transactions. One, familiar to most Americans, is the retail sales tax used by all but a handful of the states as a major revenue source. The other, used by most countries in Europe, is the value-added tax (commonly referred to as a VAT).

The difference between the two taxes is more administrative than economic. Under a retail sales tax, individuals who buy products for consumption (not businesses that buy products as inputs to their own production) pay some percentage of the retail price of the product in tax. Under the VAT, every purchaser of a product, whether business or individual, pays a tax on each transaction; but each business can claim a refund for the taxes it paid (on its purchases) against the taxes it collected (on its sales). With this string of refunds extending all the way back in the production chain, the VAT is in its net effect very similar to a national sales tax.

---

3. For example, Hausman argues that the impact on labor supply could be quite important. Jerry A. Hausman, "Labor Supply," Henry J. Aaron and Joseph A. Pechman, eds., *How Taxes Affect Economic Behavior* (Washington, D.C.: The Brookings Institution, 1981), pp. 27-72.

A VAT or a national sales tax would probably be added on to the tax system, rather than substituting completely for any existing tax.[4] On those terms, either could make a substantial dent in the deficit. The tax base (that is, the total amount of money subject to tax) would be about $3.1 trillion at 1988 levels.[5] Thus, a 10 percent VAT or sales tax might raise about $310 billion. It is quite likely, however, that the tax base would have to be significantly smaller than that theoretical maximum to make the tax fairer. A major question regarding the VAT is whether it can achieve fairness without undue complexity.

Fairness

A VAT or sales tax on all consumption would bear most heavily on people with low incomes. In technical terms, such a tax would be regressive; that is, it would take a greater share of the income of people with smaller incomes. This is because people with modest incomes tend to consume more of what they earn to maintain what they consider acceptable living standards. People with higher incomes, in contrast, can maintain a higher standard of living with only part of their incomes, and save the rest. With a sales tax falling at the same rate on all the income of the poor but on only part of the income of the wealthy, the poor would pay a greater share of their income in tax.

One frequently proposed remedy for this regressivity is to exempt consumption of "necessities"—food, housing (which would be difficult to tax anyway), medical care, perhaps clothing and utilities—from the national sales tax or VAT. The reasoning is that low-income households devote significantly more of their budgets to these necessities than do households with average and above-average income. Thus, exempting these commodities from tax is thought to relieve the burden on low-income persons.

This exemption might work for the poorest of the poor, who have little money left over after paying rent, but otherwise, it would be far less effective. Above a bare minimum of income, households divide their total spending among different general classes of commodities in roughly the same proportions.[6] The major effect of such exemptions is to shrink the tax base, so that

---

4. Either tax could replace part of the revenue now raised by the individual or corporate income taxes or by the Social Security payroll tax.

5. U.S. Department of the Treasury, *Tax Reform for Fairness, Simplicity, and Economic Growth: The Treasury Department Report to the President* (Washington, D.C.: U.S. Government Printing Office, November 1984), vol. 3, table 7-1, p. 86.

6. Ibid., pp. 89-111.

all households must pay tax on other consumption at a higher rate (or the government loses substantial revenue). Thus, exempting all food, housing, and medical care expenditures could reduce the $3.1 trillion of total consumption in the economy to a tax base of as little as $1.7 trillion.[7] So the yield of a 10 percent national sales tax or VAT with these exemptions would be not $310 billion, but as little as $170 billion.

The Complications of Low-Income Relief

Because exemptions of commodities are incomplete remedies, we could expect further efforts to undo the regressivity of national sales tax or VAT. Some VAT or sales tax advocates suggest a refundable income tax credit to make the poor and near-poor wholly exempt from the new tax. Some fraction of income assumed to be paid in sales tax would be refunded to households when they filed their federal income tax returns. The exemptions and income tax credits used for low-income relief would add considerable complexity, both to the VAT or national sales tax and to the federal income tax.

Exemptions from the tax base would complicate tax administration. Even supposedly clear-cut categories of goods and services to be exempt, such as food or medical care, have gray areas that would be difficult to rule either in or out of the tax base. There are many examples from the experience of the states with their sales taxes. Every sales-tax state exempts some expenditures, but there is an enormous degree of variation: different treatment of prepared as opposed to unprepared food, children's as opposed to adults' clothing, prescription as opposed to nonprescription drugs, among many other inconsistencies.[8] There would be the same complexities in demarcating a federal tax base. And with taxes in all the states differing in greater or lesser detail, a federal tax base obviously could be identical to only one state tax base (or the states would have to change their tax bases). In all the other states, retail sales personnel would have to know what goods were taxable under both taxes, or states would have to change their laws.

Some European governments go even further than simple exclusions and impose different tax rates on different goods and services, attempting to put

---

7. Ibid., p. 87.
8. U.S. Advisory Commission on Intergovernmental Relations, *Significant Features of Fiscal Federalism* (Washington, D.C.: U.S. Government Printing Office), 1981-82 edition, Section II; for more detail, 1979-80 edition, tables 75-80, pp. 98-108.

a heavier tax on "luxuries" than on basic goods.[9] These distinctions cause even more complication than simple exemptions alone. The distinction between a luxury item and a basic good is totally subjective, and categorizing products can be extremely contentious. Furthermore, it is difficult to carry the distinction between luxuries and basic goods all the way up and down the production chain when the same inputs can go into both. But even beyond the central determination of which goods are luxuries and which are not, the ultimate administration of the tax carries all the way down to the retail cash register. If the system is too complicated to be implemented in neighborhood stores, it necessarily will be nonuniform in application. In addition, exemptions and differential rates will introduce economic distortions in consumer choices, belying the neutrality among different goods and services that is sometimes claimed as an advantage of the national sales tax or VAT.

A refundable income tax credit to relieve the low-income burden would complicate income tax administration as well.[10] Claiming the credit would involve relatively complex computations by the low-income population. The tax credit would have to be phased out as income increased, but phasing out a tax credit (or a deduction) is one of the most complicated computations for taxpayers.

Even more significantly, such a tax credit would increase both the number of income tax returns filed and the amount of information on those returns. The refundable tax credit should go not only to persons with low incomes from wages or pensions, but also to persons receiving only welfare or Social Security benefits. Under current law, such persons need not even file tax returns; but if they are to benefit from a refundable tax credit, they would need to file. This could add millions of tax returns to the IRS workload. There are also many current tax filers who have some income from welfare or Social Security that they don't have to report on their tax returns. In fairness, those persons should have to report their benefits for purposes of determining the credit. This would be a significant complication for those taxpayers and for the IRS.

---

9. Henry J. Aaron, ed., *The Value-Added Tax: Lessons from Europe* (Washington, D.C.: The Brookings Institution, 1981). Some European governments also make a distinction between a tax exemption (meaning that no tax is collected on the sale of a product, and no refund of tax on its inputs is allowed) and "zero rating" (meaning that there is no tax on sale, but the seller can claim a refund of the tax on the inputs).

10. Some people might argue that no refundable tax credit is necessary because low-income groups receiving indexed government benefits (like Social Security) would be held harmless if prices rose. But not all benefit programs are indexed (welfare programs generally are not). The income tax exemptions, zero brackets, and earned-income tax credit could be increased to give relief to taxable persons, but it could be difficult to give adequate relief at low-income levels without losing even more revenue at upper-income levels.

Finally, even with some refundable tax credit, the VAT or national sales tax would impose a burden on low-income persons. Such persons would be forced to pay the sales tax all year long, and then wait until the year was over to file an income tax return and get their money back.[11] There is no practical way to prevent this kind of forced loan from the poor to the federal government. More frequent refunds would just multiply the paperwork, and any kind of exemption at the cash register would both complicate the tax and invite abuse.

Tax Administration

Even beyond the problems of providing low-income relief, a national sales tax or a VAT would add substantially to the IRS's administrative load. Either one would add an entirely new tax to the nation's tax system, requiring an entirely new bureaucracy to collect it. It would take time to write the new law and regulations, design and print the new forms, and hire the new workers before tax collections could begin. Businesses and tax administrators would have to document and verify millions of transactions. The administrative burden is large enough that a VAT or national sales tax might not justify its own overhead with a rate of less than 5 percent.

The choice between a VAT and a national sales tax (if such a choice were to be made) would depend largely on their relative administrative problems. A VAT would impose a paperwork burden on all businesses, while a national sales tax would affect only retailers. Because most retailers already deal with state sales taxes, the bookkeeping burden for them at least would not be entirely new; for nonretail businesses, however, compliance with a VAT would require filing new and additional forms. The number of taxable transactions under a VAT would also be much greater than the number under a national sales tax. On these grounds, a sales tax might be preferable to a VAT.

A VAT has advantages in that a refund claimed by a business purchaser requires a receipt from the seller who collected the tax; this provides a check against tax evasion on the part of the seller. A sales tax is collected entirely at the retail level, and so provides no such "audit trail." Furthermore, if a retailer successfully evades a sales tax, the entire tax is lost; if a retailer evades his share of a VAT, however, some part of the tax on his sales has still been

---

11. The same would be true of implicit relief through indexation of benefit programs and, depending on the accuracy of changes in withholding, selective income tax cuts to compensate for the VAT or national sales tax.

collected at earlier stages of the production chain. (There remains a danger of fallacious claiming of refunds under a VAT.)

Either a VAT or a national sales tax would make the fiscal relationship between the states and the federal government somewhat more difficult. The states as a group rely on retail sales taxes for about half of their tax revenue[12] (though five states have no sales tax). The states might perceive a new and substantial federal sales tax or VAT as a threat to the state sales taxes. For example, a state with a 5 or 6 percent sales tax might feel pressure to cut its tax (or feel resistance against raising it) if a new federal tax made the total rate of sales taxation 11 or 12 percent.

Inflation

Upon its introduction, a national sales tax or VAT would probably raise the average price level. Depending on the response of monetary policy, either tax could add directly to retail prices and thus to the Consumer Price Index. Later, this one-time shock could echo through the economy, either by the encouragement to workers to bargain for higher wages, or by cost-of-living adjustment provisions in preexisting labor contracts. Although inflation has been much reduced from the peaks of 1979 and 1980, we have learned in the past twenty years just how hard and painful it is to stop an ongoing inflation. Thus, even with lower inflation today, the inflationary impact of a VAT or national sales tax still might be a serious disadvantage.

Another problem with the VAT or sales tax is that it might stimulate government spending. The revenue from either would be substantial. Furthermore, because both are relatively hidden taxes, the tax rate would be a handy lever to pull to expand the federal sector.

International Trade

The VAT is sometimes supported as a potential boon to our balance of trade. Because a VAT or national sales tax probably would not be charged on exports, it is alleged that we would be more competitive in international markets. This argument does not bear scrutiny. If a VAT or national sales tax were added to our current tax system with no other change, relative prices of our exports and imports would not change. But if a VAT partly substituted for another tax, and monetary policy were loosened to avoid an economic

---

12. U.S. Department of Commerce, *Survey of Current Business*, June 1984, table 3.3, p. 9. The data in the table include federal grants-in-aid and local government tax revenues (primarily from property taxes).

contraction from the increased revenue, prices would rise, wiping out the potential trade advantage. If monetary policy were not loosened and prices remained fixed, the across-the-board price advantage would probably be offset by a higher value of the dollar than would otherwise obtain. Thus, the VAT or national sales tax should not be seen as a source of greater international competitiveness.

In sum, a VAT or national sales tax could raise a considerable amount of revenue, but it would bear most heavily on the people least able to pay, unless complex steps were taken to offset the burden. It also would add a new bureaucracy and compliance burden, would introduce its own economic distortions, and would put the federal and state governments into competition over the retail sales tax base. And it would raise the price level and might increase inflation. Finally, a VAT to narrow the deficit would leave our income tax in its present unsatisfactory state, possibly requiring further action in a few years. Hence it is probably inadvisable to add another tax to the federal revenue system, with the inevitable complications that implies, unless there is no satisfactory way to cut the deficit using existing taxes. Because a VAT or national sales tax would add to paperwork and bureaucracy, we would probably not want to add such a tax just to substitute in part for an existing tax; to be worthwile, the new tax would have to reduce the deficit as well.

Taxes on Households

The second form of consumption tax is sometimes called a personal expenditure tax or a "consumed income tax." Unlike the VAT or national sales tax, the personal expenditure tax would be collected directly from households on an annual basis. It would closely resemble the current income tax, and so would replace, rather than supplement, the income tax. This new tax would allow households to claim their own personal exemptions, replacing the complex low-income-relief devices required with the VAT or national sales tax. Nonetheless, proposals for a personal expenditure tax, like those for the sales tax or the VAT, could run aground on allegations of unfairness and complexity. Theoretical advantages of the personal expenditure tax on grounds of administrative and economic efficiency, though real, carry less weight in practice.

The Tax Deduction for Savings

To achieve the consumption tax goal of exempting capital income from tax, the personal expenditure tax would add to the current income tax a full deduction for all savings in whatever form—cash, stocks, bonds, or productive machinery or buildings. Also, the tax would require that taxpayers add to taxable income all borrowed money and all withdrawals from past savings. Until consumed, savings and accumulated interest would be completely tax free.[13]

To see that the personal expenditure tax really does exempt capital income from tax, consider an investment by a taxpayer in a 50 percent tax bracket. If the taxpayer were willing to reduce his consumption by $1,000, he could invest $2,000; his own forgone consumption would be supplemented by a $1,000 tax reduction because of the deduction for saving. With a 10 percent rate of return, the taxpayer would have $2,200 after one year. If he then withdrew his savings, paid the tax that was due, and consumed the balance, he would owe $1,100 in tax and have $1,100 left to spend; his $1,000 of deferred consumption would yield 10 percent, the before-tax rate of interest. The tax deduction in the first year is, in effect, a government-financed matching grant for saving; the tax in the second year is just the government's recouping of its matching grant, with interest. There is really no tax at all on capital income.[14]

Economic Efficiency

The personal expenditure tax has some undeniable theoretical advantages with respect to economic efficiency, but their importance in the real world is uncertain. The most common argument for the personal expenditure tax (or for facsimiles that involve expansion and liberalization of current-law Individual Retirement Accounts) is that it would increase saving. As was noted earlier, there is no theoretical or empirical backing for a substantial response of saving to tax cuts (early experience with the 1981 tax cuts, heavily

---

13. A bill to this effect was introduced in 1984 by Rep. Cecil Heltel. One alternative form of expenditure tax is the proposal of Robert E. Hall and Alvin Rabushka, introduced by Sen. Dennis DeConcini. This tax allows no deduction for saving but does not tax any income from capital, thus obviously achieving the tax exemption. Another approach is a bill introduced by Sen. William Roth and Rep. Henson Moore, which allows a maximum $10,000 deduction for saving ($20,000 for couples), but does not tax borrowed money. This last proposal would allow creditworthy taxpayers to borrow $10,000 and then redeposit it just to get the tax deduction, a significant disadvantage.

14. The outcome could vary from this simple model if the income were consumed in a tax-rate bracket different from that in which it was deducted. Also, this process could be viewed in a different way. Consider two taxpayers who invested the same amount in one year and consumed the proceeds in the next year, but only one made a successful investment. In effect, because of the deduction for saving and taxation of ultimate consumption, the federal government would share the gain of the one taxpayer, because that person's taxable consumption would exceed the deduction for saving; but the government would also share the loss of the other taxpayer, because that person's deduction for saving would exceed the taxable consumption.

focused on capital income, lends little support), and the benefits for the economy from a feasible increase in personal saving are probably modest.

Far more valid, though certainly far less compelling, are arguments that the personal expenditure tax reduces economic distortions. The most important is the choice between present and future consumption. The example just cited showed that the rate of return on forgone consumption under the expenditure tax is the same as the market rate of interest. In contrast, people who save under the income tax pay tax on the money they earn and on the return to their savings; there is a "wedge" between the market and the after-tax rate of return.[15] This distorts taxpayers' choices between spending today and saving to spend later. As was noted earlier, it is not certain that taxpayers would save more under an expenditure tax, but their decision would be based on the market rate of return without the interference of the tax system.

Administrative Advantage of the Personal Expenditure Tax

The immediate deduction of saving and investment gives the personal expenditure tax several administrative advantages in the measurement of income from capital. One example is the handling of depreciation of investments in physical capital (machines or buildings). Under an income tax, the cost of such an investment must be deducted gradually, over the expected lifetime of the particular asset. Inflation erodes the value of those deductions, however; by the time an asset is fully depreciated for tax purposes, the cost of replacing it is greater than the historical cost that was deducted, and so the investor gets less than the original investment back. To compensate, the tax law allows accelerated depreciation—that is, deduction of the asset's cost over less than its useful life, or with larger deductions in the early years, or both. Through accelerated depreciation, an investor can recover the investment sooner and can reinvest it, making up some ground against inflation. The Accelerated Cost Recovery System (ACRS), part of the 1981 tax cuts, the current version of accelerated depreciation, is the most rapidly accelerated depreciation ever allowed under the U.S. income tax.

There are two problems with accelerated depreciation. One is that it requires recordkeeping from year to year to keep track of the amounts deducted in the past and deductible in the future. Such recordkeeping can be quite complex. Second, the degree of acceleration allowed is generally a hit-or-miss affair, either over- or under-compensating for inflation whenever the

---

15. In the foregoing example, the taxpayer would be able to save only $1,000. The interest income in one year would be $100, half of which would have to be paid in tax. So the after-tax rate of return would be 5 percent ($50 divided by $1000), even though the market rate of interest was 10 percent.

price level fluctuates. The only alternative is to index the basis of depreciable assets for inflation, increasing the as-yet undepreciated balance each year for the increase in the price level. This process adds complexity to depreciation accounting and makes the nominal dollar amount of the deduction in any given year uncertain when businesses are trying to plan their investment strategies.

The immediate deduction of investment costs in the expenditure tax eliminates these problems. There is no uncertainty about the amount to be deducted in future years, because the entire deduction is taken immediately. And inflation cannot influence the real value of the deduction, because the deduction is taken immediately, before inflation can act upon it. Furthermore, all investments are treated the same, and there is no unintended advantage of one type of investment over others.

The distorting effects of inflation and the advantage of the expenditure tax extend to the financial investments (such as stocks and bonds) of households as well as to the physical investments of businesses. Thus, an investor might receive 10 percent interest on a bond at a time when the inflation rate is 10 percent. The interest merely compensates the investor for the depreciation of the principal invested in the bond, but all of that 10 percent interest is taxed anyway under an income tax; so there is a tax even though there is no real income. The same kind of mismeasurement of income can occur with capital gains. Solving this problem under the income tax, again, requires a very complex "tax base indexation"—recomputing all capital income and all interest expense to express all money amounts in inflation-adjusted dollars. (Indexation of the income tax base is discussed in more detail in the next chapter.)

The personal expenditure tax deals with these problems by taxing consumption rather than income. If two persons each consumed a certain number of dollars in a given year, they would pay the same tax, regardless of whether one earned the money through labor and the other through investment, or one got his money by investing $1,000 well and the other by investing $10,000 poorly. The effect of inflation would be irrelevant to the personal expenditure tax base, because consumption is always measured in current dollars. (Exemptions and rate brackets would still need to be indexed to achieve complete inflation neutrality.)

So the measurement of capital income is simpler under the personal expenditure tax, and in theory, the tax is perfectly neutral among different capital investments. But in practice, neutrality (and greater revenue yield) also would require the elimination of the many targeted tax subsidies and incentives in the current law which favor particular industries and even owner-occupied housing. It is an open question, more political than economic, whether the Congress would be more likely to repeal these tax preferences in creating a new personal expenditure tax or in restructuring the current income tax. Some personal expenditure tax advocates argue for starting from scratch rather than struggling with the existing law. But beneficiaries of current preferences know what they want, and might use the transition to a new law as an occasion to bargain for new and more generous preferences. There is no way to know how such a political process would end.

Fairness

The theoretical neutrality of the personal expenditure tax among investments is not surprising, considering that capital income is effectively tax exempt (as was explained earlier). There is no tax to distort choices among investments, and no tax with which inflation can interact. These advantages are nothing to sneeze at. Nonetheless, the complete tax exemption for capital causes some serious problems.

The central issue is the fairness of eliminating the taxation of income from capital. In all likelihood, the American public might well reject a system that eliminated taxation of income from property and put the entire tax burden on labor. We have taxed income from both capital and labor since the income tax was adopted in 1913. A personal expenditure tax thus would be the sharpest reversal from the tax principles that the public has come to hold—taxation according to ability to pay, measured by total income. If enacted as part of a remedy to the current budget crunch, the personal expenditure tax would lift the tax burden from capital and shift it to labor at the same time as the *total* tax burden was increased to reduce the deficit—so owners of property would get a break while working people would experience a double tax increase. This might strike many taxpayers as unfair.

The unfairness of the tax exemption for capital income would manifest itself in several ways. For one thing, the typical taxpayer's burden would be shifted to different parts of the life span. Under the income tax, people pay their highest taxes when they earn their highest incomes—typically middle age, the peak earning years. An expenditure tax would change that. Taxpayers would pay relatively more in their early working years, when people usually borrow to set up households, and in retirement, when people typically spend much or all of their accumulated savings. Taxes in the peak earning years would be relatively lighter than they are now. Under the principles of the personal expenditure tax, this pattern is perfectly logical; people should pay less tax when they save, and more when they borrow or dissave. But from the popular viewpoint, such a shift of taxes could seem illogical and unfair. The tax burden would be shifted away from the time of the greatest ability to pay.

For the same reasons, the personal expenditure tax would shift the tax burden from people's good times to their bad times. If someone loses a job or becomes ill and has to draw on past savings, the personal expenditure tax would make those withdrawals from savings taxable. Savings out of windfall income, however, would be tax exempt. These changes likely would be counterintuitive to most taxpayers, and certainly counter to their ability to pay.

The Concentration of Wealth

The end result of a changeover to a personal expenditure tax, all else being equal, would be an increase in the concentration of holdings of wealth. People who now have the most income and wealth would have the greatest opportunity to save more. If the personal expenditure tax had graduated tax rates, the wealthy would also get the largest government matching grants for every dollar they saved. Their wealth would accumulate from year to year without tax, and would be passed on to their heirs, after only modest estate taxes, to continue to accumulate without tax. In the long run, there could be economic, political, and social dangers to such accumulations of wealth and power.

One option for limiting the concentration of wealth under a personal expenditure tax would be taxing all (or all above some minimum amount) of a taxpayer's gifts and bequests as though they were consumption.[16] Thus, some or all savings and any accumulated interest would be added to the taxpayer's consumption on a final tax return when the taxpayer died. In theory, this makes perfect sense. If people choose to give away their money rather than to spend it on themselves, they must get at least as much satisfaction from their gifts as from their spending; so in that sense, the taxpayers are consuming their income even if they give it away. Furthermore, if all accumulated savings and interest were taxed at death, that would mean that taxable consumption over a taxpayer's lifetime would equal precisely all of

---

16. This is an important element of the personal expenditure tax variant called a "lifetime income tax" proposed by Henry J. Aaron and Harvey Galper, "Reforming the Tax System," in Alice M. Rivlin, *Economic Choices 1984* (Washington, D.C.: The Brookings Institution, 1984), pp. 87-117. In fact, Aaron and Galper write that "If gifts and bequests are not included in the . . . tax base . . . a wholly different approach to tax reform may well be preferable" (p. 116).

the person's income; omitting gifts and requests would mean that some income would escape taxation.

The problem with taxing gifts and bequests as consumption is that by all precedents it would be extremely unpopular. The American people have a strong bias against taxation upon death. The federal estate tax has never raised substantial amounts of revenue, and its base has at least as many leakages as the income tax's.[17] Efforts to reform or increase the estate tax have met extreme opposition, and in 1981 the estate tax was sharply cut back. An attempt to incorporate some accounting for accumulated wealth in the annual income tax—the so-called "carryover basis" provision for inherited assets on which capital gains have accrued—failed after a protracted legislative battle. In addition, special provisions would be needed to tax people who earned their incomes and saved in the United States, and then took their money to spend (perhaps in retirement) overseas. Finally, even personal expenditure tax advocates are sharply divided on this issue; some argue against any form of wealth taxation, on the ground that it would discourage saving, while others view taxation of gifts and bequests as essential for fairness. Thus, a personal expenditure tax would increase the concentration of the ownership of wealth unless there were significant changes in attitudes toward taxation of wealth (possibly at death) and in other parts of the tax system. Because the personal expenditure tax couples a greater long-run concentration of wealth with appearances of unfairness on a year-by-year basis, the public would probably oppose such a tax.

The Personal Expenditure Tax and the Budget Deficit

The exemption for capital income in the personal expenditure tax causes still further problems with respect to both the budget deficit and tax administration. Because the personal expenditure tax would start from the income tax base and then allow a deduction for saving, there would simply be fewer dollars to be taxed. Thus, the personal expenditure tax would start the deficit reduction drive with a handicap. Of course, the ultimate size of the tax base for the personal expenditure tax would depend also on the disposition of the many tax preferences in the current law. As was noted earlier, repealing tax preferences may be no easier under a personal expenditure tax than under the current income tax, and because of the deduction for saving, more preferences would have to be repealed under a personal expenditure tax.

---

17. George Cooper, *A Voluntary Tax? New Perspectives on Sophisticated Estate Tax Avoidance* (Washington, D.C.: The Brookings Institution, 1979).

The revenue handicap of the personal expenditure tax would be even greater at its adoption than in the long run. In the simplest terms, a person who earns income this year and spends it next year would pay tax this year under the income tax but next year under the expenditure tax. Under the current income tax system, many people have saved out of fully taxed income. From the expenditure tax point of view these people paid tax too soon; they should pay only when they spend their income. In this simple example, if an expenditure tax replaced an income tax between the two years, people would pay tax on their income in the first year, and again on what remained when they spent it in the second year. In fact, if we enacted a personal expenditure tax without special provisions for transition, savers would have to pay tax on their past savings all over again when they withdrew and spent them. This would be particularly hard on older workers near retirement; all of their past taxable savings, including money put into bank accounts, stocks, and bonds, would be taxed all over again when they withdrew and spent it. This burden clearly would be intolerable, and so there would have to be provisions for relief.

The only correct form of relief would be to take an inventory of all past savings, and allow tax deductions for all savings made out of taxable income— but not for tax-deferred savings, like IRAs or employer-paid pensions.[18] Creating such balance sheets and distinguishing among different kinds of savings would be an enormous administrative task. Beyond tax administration, however, these provisions for transition relief would pose a major revenue problem. At a time when the federal government is seriously short of revenue, the transition to a personal expenditure tax would require what is, in effect, a refund of past taxes. So with ongoing revenue costs in terms of the added deduction for saving, and an added revenue cost during the transition, the personal expenditure tax as a deficit reduction fighter would have both hands tied behind its back. Tax rates would have to be higher, and higher tax rates would discourage work effort.[19] Furthermore, the actual revenue yield of a personal expenditure tax, and the revenue cost of the transition basis adjustments are unpredictable; precise data on either current or past saving by

---

18. Such balance sheets would be needed also to prevent the concealment of wealth at the time of transition to the expenditure tax. Concealed wealth could later be deposited as though it were new saving for a tax deduction, or consumed without tax.

19. Furthermore, if people with higher incomes tend to save greater proportions of their income, as is believed to be the case, tax rates under a personal expenditure tax would have to be more steeply graduated than those under an income tax, as well as higher, to achieve the same progressivity of tax liabilities as the income tax.

household income groups do not exist.[20] Finally, although the transition basis adjustments make perfect sense from a personal expenditure tax perspective, many people would consider it unfair for wealthy taxpayers to receive large tax deductions because they saved at some time in the past.

Tax Administration Disadvantages

The tax deduction for saving would lead to some administrative problems. All taxpayers, even those with low incomes, would have to account for their savings as well as for their borrowings under the personal expenditure tax. This would be an entirely new compliance burden, akin to itemizing deductions for the two-thirds of taxpayers who now may claim the simpler standard deduction. Furthermore, paying tax on borrowings would be an entirely new financial burden. Unless there were withholding on borrowings, taxpayers who took out loans might find that they owed extra taxes at the end of the year. Despite its complexity and probable unpopularity, this part of the personal expenditure tax could not be omitted; failure to tax borrowed money would allow unlimited tax avoidance, as creditworthy persons could borrow money tax free, and then deposit those funds to claim tax deductions. This change in the tax treatment of borrowed money would require a virtual re-education of all individual taxpayers.

Taxing Corporations under a Personal Expenditure Tax

The corporate income tax plays an uncertain role under the income tax system. Its major function is to prevent individuals from transferring money to corporations, to earn interest there free of tax. The corporate tax causes economic distortions by discouraging incorporation and inducing movements of capital out of the corporate sector.

Under a personal expenditure tax, there is no need for a corporate income tax. If expenditure, rather than income, is to be taxed, corporations should not pay any expenditure tax because corporations do not consume.

Furthermore, under a personal expenditure tax, there is no need for a corporate tax to protect the personal tax. A corporation would merely allow the tax-free accumulation of capital income; but under a personal expenditure tax, capital income would not be taxed until it was consumed anyway. Thus,

---

20. Household surveys on consumption conducted for the Labor Department to choose the "market basket" for the Consumer Price Index yield saving data as a residual. These surveys are designed to reflect the typical consumer, however, and are less accurate for people with low or particularly high income.

individuals would not need corporation as tax shelters, because their own bank accounts would work just as well.

Of course, abolishing the corporate income tax would cause a loss of revenue. To make up the loss, the personal expenditure tax would have to raise additional revenue, presumably through higher rates. To suggest rough orders of magnitude, current projected revenues for 1989 are about $500 billion for the individual income tax and about $100 billion for the corporate income tax;[21] so a personal expenditure tax that raised revenue equal to the individual income tax would need a 20 percent across-the-board rate increase (or some equivalent) to replace the revenues of the corporate tax.

Some personal expenditure tax advocates would keep a form of corporate tax to maintain revenue or to prevent a windfall to owners of existing corporations (whose market values are now set in the expectation of future corporate tax liabilities). One approach would be an excise tax on corporate profits, independent of the personal expenditure tax. Such a tax would discourage incorporation, because unincorporated businesses would not have to pay. Another approach would be a cash-flow tax. Corporations would expense all their investments, deduct all other costs from their cash flow, and pay a tax on the balance. Under the cash-flow tax, firms that earned a normal rate of return would pay no net tax over time because their deductions for investment would offset their net income (much as individuals would pay no net tax on capital income under a personal expenditure tax), but firms earning supernormal returns would pay tax. (The tax would also reach returns on investments made before the personal expenditure tax was introduced.)

To personal expenditure tax purists, such a tax would be excessive, in that it would be paid in addition to individuals' taxes on their consumption. Like an excise on corporate profits, a cash-flow tax would discourage incorporation, because supernormal returns earned by unincorporated businesses would not be subject to a separate tax. Thus, any corporate tax under a personal expenditure tax would have no theoretical role to play and would be retained only because of revenue needs. To many advocates, one of the major advantages of the personal expenditure tax is the ease of repealing the corporate income tax. But because the deficit crisis and the revenue handicaps of the personal expenditure tax (its deduction for saving in the long run, and the need for basis adjustment deductions for past saving in the short run) would cause serious revenue pressure, this advantage probably would be lost.

---

21. Congressional Budget Office, *The Economic and Budget Outlook: An Update* (Washington, D.C.: U.S. Government Printing Office, August 1984), table III-3, p. 57.

As was noted earlier, the personal expenditure tax would eliminate some complicated aspects of the tax law, including business depreciation accounting and computation of capital gain or loss (because the entire proceeds of sales of capital assets would be taxable if not reinvested). Although these simplifications are significant, they affect only businesses, which generally use professional accountants, and a minority of individual taxpayers, generally only the most affluent and educated. In contrast, the tax deduction for saving and taxability of borrowing would affect all taxpayers, including those least able to handle any additional complication.

Conclusion

In sum, the personal expenditure tax has theoretical advantages, but also practical shortcomings that are especially significant in a deficit reduction role. The personal expenditure tax is commonly billed as an incentive for saving, but its potential in that regard is probably limited. If the personal expenditure tax is enacted in its pure form, it is completely neutral among different types of investments. The tax also eliminates the mismeasurement of capital income because of inflation, and it significantly simplifies depreciation accounting. But it would accomplish these valuable goals by, in effect, completely eliminating the tax on capital income (in the absence of an unlikely additional tax on wealth)—a step that would probably be considered unfair, especially if, at the same time, total taxes, newly loaded entirely onto labor income, had to be increased. A correct transition to the personal expenditure tax would require a monumental accounting for all past savings, and a deduction for past fully taxed savings. Otherwise, those savings would be double-taxed when they were consumed—especially unfair for people now approaching retirement. These necessary transition deductions would cost revenue, as would the ongoing deductions for saving—particularly inopportune now, when the budget deficit is rewriting the record books. Finally, the personal expenditure tax would change fundamental tax concepts to which taxpayers have become accustomed over the seventy-year history of the income tax, and would require more reporting of information.

The personal expenditure tax would be more attractive if the federal government could afford to lose revenue and could take several years for a slow and painstaking transition. But with the current large budget deficits, any transition to a new tax system must be accomplished quickly and with no loss of revenue. Under these circumstances, the disadvantages of the personal expenditure tax may be overwhelming, despite its advantages—particularly its potential neutrality—in other respects.

Summary

Despite their similar rationale, the two types of expenditure tax would play distinctly different roles in the federal revenue system: the value-added tax or national sales tax would supplement existing taxes to raise revenue; and the personal expenditure tax would replace the individual and corporate income taxes.

A VAT or a national sales tax would have considerable potential to raise revenue but would be less attractive on other grounds. Many of its disadvantages would be administrative: it would add another layer of paperwork and bureaucracy to the revenue system, and it would require a complex refund scheme to relieve what many people would call an excessive burden on low-income taxpayers.

Although a personal expenditure tax would replace existing taxes, it would involve complexity of its own. The transition to a personal expenditure tax would be extremely difficult and would cost revenue. Furthermore, the personal expenditure tax would impose new paperwork burdens on individual taxpayers and would require a virtual reeducation of the mass of taxpayers regarding the expenditure tax principles of taxing borrowed money and not taxing savings.

The most common rationale for taxing consumption in any form is to encourage saving. But as both our recent experience and our institutions suggest, we are unlikely to increase household saving significantly through tax policy, and the impact on our economy of any increase in saving would be modest. The personal expenditure tax has certain virtues in theory, but its practical weaknesses reduce its appeal. And although a VAT or a national sales tax could be a last-resort choice to reduce the deficit, it would exact a heavy toll in administrative terms.

CHAPTER 6

MAKING THE SHORT LIST: TAXING INCOME

The income tax system has serious flaws, but so do all the alternatives. Consumption taxes entail painful costs of transition; distribute their burdens in ways that could be seen as unfair, at least from the perspective of the current system; and have limited benefits in terms of economic growth and efficiency.

But we should not resort to simple increases in income tax rates to reduce the deficit. Rate increases would be unfair, so long as some people pay too little and others too much tax; tax-rate increases pass over the people who already avoid tax, and bear heavily on those who now pay too much. Higher rates also exacerbate any economic distortions caused by the income tax.

The remaining option is to work within the structure of the current income tax. Income tax restructuring or reform requires broadening the base of income subject to tax by eliminating or restricting many of the deductions, exclusions, and credits available under the current law. Tax restructuring can increase tax revenues by broadening the base, so that tax rates can be reduced in partial compensation while the budget deficit is narrowed. In contrast to the all-out warfare of introducing an entirely new tax, restructuring the income tax can limit conflict to particular tax law provisions that narrow the tax base, make the system complex and unfair, and distort economic decisions. But a lot of these provisions would have to be eliminated or cut back—far more than in the 1982 or 1984 tax bills—to achieve this ambitious goal.

The Individual Income Tax

Dimensions of a Restructured Income Tax

Some rough calculations will illustrate the potential and the prerequisites of tax restructuring. In 1982, taxpayers reported roughly $1.917 trillion of

103

income on their tax returns, with $1.865 trillion on taxable returns (see table 9). After about $61 billion for statutory adjustments to income, $191 billion of personal exemptions, and $170 billion for itemized deductions, there was about $1.446 trillion of taxable income on the returns. With $221 billion of that income falling into the zero brackets (and therefore taxed at a zero tax rate), there remained $1.225 trillion taxed at "nonzero" tax rates, raising about $278 billion in revenue (after about $7 billion of tax credits). At 1984 tax rates, the revenue would be about $248 billion.

Income tax restructuring requires substantially increasing the amount of income subject to tax —perhaps by one-fifth, which would be $250 billion at 1982 income levels. Then tax rates could be reduced by one-sixth on average (though the precise pattern would depend on how much the taxable incomes of different income groups increased) with no loss of revenue. The $250 billion of additional taxable income would come from two sources: by increasing the $1.917 trillion of income reported and by decreasing the $692

TABLE 9

THE INDIVIDUAL INCOME TAX BASE, 1982
(*In trillions of current dollars*)

Gross income, all returns		$1.917
less:	Gross income, nontaxable returns	0.052
equals:	Gross income, taxable returns	1.865
less:	Statutory adjustments to income	0.061
equals:	Adjusted gross income, taxable returns	1.804
less:	Personal exemptions (dollar amount)	0.191
	Excess itemized deductions	0.170
equals:	Taxable income on taxable returns[a]	1.446
less:	Zero-bracket amounts[a]	0.221
equals:	Income taxed at "nonzero" rates	1.225
Tax before credits[b]		0.285
less:	Tax credits	0.007
equals:	Total income tax	0.278

SOURCES: U.S. Department of the Treasury, Internal Revenue Service, *Statistics of Income— 1982, Individual Income Tax Returns* (Washington, D.C.: U.S. Government Printing Office, 1984), and unpublished IRS data.

NOTE: Items may not add to totals because of rounding.

a. Includes unused zero-bracked amount (equal to $2 billion).
b. Includes minimum tax and alternative minimum tax.

billion of reported income not subject to tax (that is, the difference between gross income on all returns and income taxed at "non-zero" rates). Revenue also could be gained by reducing the $7 billion of tax credits.

Increasing reported incomes requires bringing legally exempt income into the tax base (or tapping the underground economy, an achievement that cannot be counted on). If deductions from gross income did not increase, an increase of about 13 percent of gross income would meet this target. Reducing itemized tax deductions and statutory exclusions cannot contribute as much to the process, simply because the amount of deductions and exclusions is much smaller. In 1982, itemized deductions and adjustments to income could have been eliminated without increasing taxable income by 20 percent.

In fact, tax restructuring would probably exempt at least some income that is now taxable. As was noted in chapter 2, inflation has significantly eroded the personal exemptions and zero-bracket amounts since they were last increased in 1978. Any significant revision of the income tax would have to include an upward revision of the exemptions and zero-bracket amounts to ease this burden on low-income taxpayers. This would require a further broadening of the income base and pruning of the deductions and exclusions.

Several restructuring proposals submitted to the Congress since 1982 would have repealed some deductions and statutory exclusions, broadened the definition of income, and increased relief for low-income taxpayers. These proposals would have fully replaced current tax revenues using maximum rates of 30 percent, in contrast to the 50 percent in the current law. This change represents about a 20 percent increase in the overall size of the tax base. If we express the effects of the two recent tax laws as percentage increases of the tax base, the 1982 tax increase achieved about 4 percent and the 1984 bill about 3 percent.[1]

The potential additional taxable income is there. According to estimates by the Congressional Joint Tax Committee, well over $200 billion of tax revenue will be lost through tax expenditures in fiscal 1985.[2] Nonetheless, that figure almost certainly overstates the potential for broadening the tax base.

---

1. Congressional Budget Office, *Reducing the Deficit: Spending and Revenue Options* (Washington, D.C.: U.S. Government Printing Office, February 1983), tables X-1 and X-2, pp. 228 and 230; *The Economic and Budget Outlook: An Update* (Washington, D.C.: U.S. Government Printing Office, August 1983), table 25, p. 95; and *The Economic and Budget Outlook: An Update* (Washington, D.C.: U.S. Government Printing Office, August 1984), tables III-3 and III-4, pp. 57-58.

2. Joint Committee on Taxation, *Estimates of Federal Tax Expenditures for Fiscal Years 1984-1989* (Washington, D.C.: U.S. Government Printing Office, November 9, 1984), table 1, pp. 9-16.

Even with reductions in tax rates, there would be little or no political support for repealing tax expenditures that relieve hardship (such as Social Security benefits for the low-income elderly, or welfare or food stamp benefits). Furthermore, repealing the hardship preferences would raise little revenue. Some other tax preferences—such as the mortgage interest deduction—have existed so long, and underlie so many long-term commitments, that removing them from the tax system would cause serious dislocations. And all tax preferences have beneficiaries with an interest in their continuation. The delicate political task is to find and repeal enough tax provisions that are inefficient at accomplishing their stated goals, or that pursue goals of low priority, and to use the revenue so gained to narrow the deficit and reduce tax rates. Given the constituency politics and the amounts of revenue involved, this task will not be easy. But the payoff, both in deficit reduction and in tax policy goals, could be significant.

Simplification

The need for revenue is one reason to repeal tax preferences, but there are others. Large numbers of tax expenditures have been added to the tax code —there were 50 in 1967, and 104 in 1983[3]—but repeals have been rare. The many exceptions to general tax rules complicate and lengthen the law, the forms, and the instructions.

As was discussed in chapter 4, the tax return of the average taxpayer is probably about as simple as we can make it; the fruits of tax simplification are more subtle. For one thing, simplification could be felt not in tax filing but in economic affairs in general. Some tax preferences are so generous that taxpayers review and alter their investments to obtain the maximum tax benefits. Without the preferences, taxpayers could make deals more on the basis of business considerations (which they have to understand anyway) and less for tax reasons, simplifying decision making.

In addition, taxpayers today have to examine all the potentially beneficial provisions in the law—deductions, exclusions, and credits—to learn if they can use them—even if in the end they cannot. Broadening the tax base would change that by reducing the number of taxpayer options, forms, and pages of instructions.

Some base-broadening steps would actually complicate the tax system; if income currently untaxed becomes taxable, more paperwork will be re-

---

3. Congressional Budget Office, *Tax Expenditures: Budget Control Options and Five-Year Projections for Fiscal Years 1983-1987* (Washington, D.C.: U.S. Government Printing Office, November 1982), p. xiv.

quired. One prominent example would be taxation of employer-provided fringe benefits. But at least in this example, the complication would rest with the employer, who would be more able to deal with it. The employer would compute and report taxable, noncash compensation to the employee, just as employers now do with cash compensation. Overall, though, eliminating such a tax preference simplifies rather than complicates economic choices. Taxpayers need no longer fine-tune their choices to minimize their tax liabilities; they need only choose the compensation package that they consider most favorable.

So simplifying the income tax would require the repeal of many tax provisions. Most taxpayers would see no difference in the tax forms that they themselves fill out or in the tax provisions that they use. What they would see is a reduction in the mass of law, regulations, forms, and instructions that they cannot or are afraid to use, but that other taxpayers have been using to reduce their taxes. The entire tax system would be cut down to a size that most taxpayers could begin to grasp.

Fairness

Broadening the income tax base, even without increasing total revenue, would raise taxes for some users of the terminated tax preferences. Is this fair?

Raising anyone's taxes is painful; no one wants to adjust to a tighter budget. Similarly, no one wants to be singled out for special treatment—if the treatment is painful. But the reshuffling of tax liabilities must be considered in the context of the current law. The consensus of the American people, as was documented in the first chapter, is that the income tax is unfair; some taxpayers pay too little and others pay too much. If this unfairness is to be remedied, those who pay too little will have to pay more.

Unfairness is perceived in the income tax because people with the same income can pay very different amounts of tax; and people with higher incomes sometimes pay smaller shares of their incomes than people who have lower incomes. This inequity arises not from graduated tax rates and personal exemptions but from the other deductions, exclusions, and credits in the tax law.

Choosing the tax preferences to repeal, again, is a judgment call requiring compromises among groups with conflicting interests. But a restructured income tax would have a "cushion" in its lower marginal tax rates against the pain of those who lose their tax preferences. People who would face substantial tax increases at least would have lower rates on any additional income they generated. Thus, over time, affected taxpayers at least would find it easier to make up their lost ground. Taxpayers who now incur expenses (such as fees of tax shelter brokers) in the course of minimizing their taxes would at least save those expenses to offset partially any increase in taxes. Finally, low tax rates may make it easier for policymakers to say no when interest groups request special treatment; with lower rates, claims of hardship status may be less persuasive. Thus, it may be easier to maintain a uniform, fair system in the future.

Economic Efficiency

Experts agree that our income tax system somewhat reduces economic growth, as was documented in chapter 3; but any administrable and equitable tax system will reduce growth and efficiency to some extent. Furthermore, although some tax alternatives (including the personal expenditure tax) would promote economic efficiency in theory, experts do not agree on what would work in practice by achieving popular acceptance and attaining fairness and simplicity as well. And as was noted earlier in this chapter, the income tax has its own structural problems, particularly in dealing with inflation.

Nonetheless, there is some agreement that the income tax can be improved. Moreover, administrative problems in the transition to a restructured income tax are at least more manageable than conversion to a personal expenditure tax.

The potential increases in efficiency come from reducing marginal tax rates and other sources of economic distortions. Rate reductions increase incentives for work and investment, but there is sharp disagreement about how much taxpayers would respond. Considering the other benefits of lower marginal rates—including reduced incentives for tax evasion and sheltering, and reductions in economic distortions induced elsewhere in the income tax— virtually all experts would prefer lower tax rates, all else being equal.

The restructured income tax would reduce distortions directly as well. Elimination and reduction of sectoral tax subsidies and incentives would allow resources to flow where the market, rather than the tax law, dictates. Allocation of resources without government interference unambiguously yields greater national income in the long run.

In two other respects, the restructured income tax would reduce but not completely eliminate economic distortions. The income tax does not measure capital income properly in periods of rapid inflation, as was mentioned earlier. The personal expenditure tax would achieve completely neutral treatment of capital by taxing only consumption, always measured in current dollars. Similarly, the income tax inevitably has what some experts consider a double tax on saving, while the personal expenditure tax does not. A restructured income tax base might be indexed for inflation. Otherwise, the lower tax rates in a restructured income tax would reduce these economic distortions. Of course, the personal expenditure tax eliminates these distortions of tax treatment of income from capital by effectively exempting such income from tax. But doing that would raise questions of tax fairness, reduce tax revenue, and increase the tax burden on labor. In the final analysis, the issue is which bundle of advantages and disadvantages is preferable.

So income tax restructuring can increase economic efficiency. All things considered, a tax increase with tax restructuring could be a net economic plus, not a minus—because of reduced deficits and interest rates, a more favorable foreign trade environment, reduced distortions, and lower marginal tax rates.

Cats and Dogs and Cats and Dogs and . . .

Some people argue that we can approach a restructured income tax over several years with a series of ''cats and dogs'' base-broadening and revenue-raising bills like those of 1982 and 1984. Unfortunately, such a process of incremental reform probably would not work.

For one thing, the deficit is nearly out of hand and needs comprehensive action. We may not be able to wait for several ''cats and dogs'' bills.

A second problem is that the ''cats and dogs'' captured in the 1982 and 1984 roundups were the slowest of the strays—instances of clear-cut abuse, inefficiency, or excessive generosity in the law. Even at that, withholding on interest and dividends was repealed from the 1982 law. The next round of tax preferences could not include such easy targets, because they have already been taken. Instead, the next round must include preferences with some rationale and more powerful constituencies. These are the kinds of preferences that can be repealed only with significant compensating rate cuts; but incremental reform bills raise too little revenue to allow rate cuts.

Finally, legislating incremental reforms could be too painful. Because small numbers of individual interest groups are singled out to receive the pain, they have the stage to themselves to argue their positions.

So we cannot pick up occasional strays while the other animals run loose and multiply. If we want to clear the streets, we will have to do it once and for all.

Conclusion

The cost of greater tax neutrality, simplicity, and fairness is a potentially painful adjustment for currently subsidized taxpayers. Even with lower marginal rates and greater long-term growth, some businesses and individuals would suffer in the short run. The question is whether the ultimate benefits are worth the short-term costs. If the income tax is to be retained, several pertinent issues must be resolved.

Inflation and the Income Tax

Some analysts argue that rapid inflation caused the deterioration of the income tax system. Chapter 2 showed how inflation affected the distribution of the tax burden by eroding the personal exemptions and standard deductions and pushing taxpayers into higher tax-rate brackets. The further problem of distortion of the measurement of business and investment income due to inflation is solved structurally by the personal expenditure tax but is much harder to deal with under the income tax. This issue is important enough to have its own discussion.

As was discussed in the preceding chapter, capital income is mismeasured during inflation because the income accrues over a long period after the investment is made. Whatever the form of the investment, the effect of inflation is similar. If a taxpayer buys a bond, part of the interest is needed to offset inflation's erosion of the principal, but *all* the interest is subject to income tax. When a taxpayer sells a share of stock (or any other asset) for a capital gain, some of that gain implicitly compensates for inflation's erosion of the original investment, but all the gain is subject to tax. Finally, depreciation of investments in business plant and equipment based on historical cost does not allow recovery of the replacement cost after inflation.[4]

This overtaxation due to mismeasurement of capital income during inflation caused numerous changes in the tax law, including the Accelerated Cost Recovery System (ACRS) in 1981 and the increase in the capital gains exclusion in 1978. These changes were intended to offset the overtaxation. What they really did, however, was to provide untargeted benefits to owners of capital; they did not, except in rare instances and by pure chance, undo even a close approximation of inflation's effects. In the process, these provisions created opportunities for abuse that have eroded the integrity of the income tax.

For example, ACRS gives accelerated deductions in part to compensate for inflation. The cost-recovery schedules allow deductions faster than an asset actually wears out; thus, implicitly, the owner could put the tax deduc-

---

4. Businesses that borrow to finance their investments receive a compensating benefit through inflation's erosion of the real value of their debts.

tions into an interest-bearing account that would grow to the replacement cost of the asset by the time it does wear out. The deduction schedules do not change, however, no matter what the inflation rate. Furthermore, economic research on the subject indicates that the degree of acceleration is greater for some assets than for others. Thus, effective tax rates under ACRS, assuming 6 percent inflation, average 15.8 percent for all assets, but range from 3.5 percent for equipment to 36.3 percent for structures.[5] ACRS is more generous than true depreciation; this greater generosity can be manipulated to create tax shelter investments, and such investments have been booming since ACRS was passed. The investment tax credit (ITC) for investments in equipment (not for buildings) is an additional subsidy also intended in part as compensation for inflation.

Similarly, 60 percent of long-term capital gains is excludable from adjusted gross income, in part as compensation for the effects of inflation. Of course, such a fixed percentage cannot be correct for every transaction at whatever rate of inflation. No percentage exclusion can be correct for a "wash" sale of an asset (that is, with a zero gain) held during a period of inflation, for example; if there is no nominal gain to exclude, there is no compensation for the loss of real purchasing power. At the same time, the exclusion affords undeserved benefits for ordinary income that is converted into capital gain through economically meaningless accounting devices; that is the essence of many tax shelter schemes.

Thus, these rough-justice adjustments for inflation are inaccurate and have undesirable side effects. The abuse of these provisions has fed the growing public dissatisfaction with the income tax. Responding to both the inaccuracy of the adjustments and the unhappiness of the public, some economists have argued for precise indexation of capital income to undo the effects of inflation.

Indexation would require an asset-by-asset correction of amounts of income and capital gain to remove the effects of inflation. For every bond and savings account, taxpayers would claim an amount of negative income for the depreciation of the invested principal. For every sale of a capital asset, taxpayers would have to convert the price they paid for the asset into current dollars before computing the capital gain. For each depreciable business asset,

---

5. Charles R. Hulten and James W. Robertson, "Corporate Tax Policy," Changing Domestic Priorities Discussion Paper (Washington, D.C.: The Urban Institute, October 1983), table IV, p. 32. The "effective tax rate" on an asset is the tax burden on the income it generates, at an assumed real rate of return and an assumed inflation rate, taking into account the acceleration of depreciation allowances and the investment tax credit in the law.

taxpayers would have to increase the remaining undepreciated balance of the asset's cost before deducting part of it. This would involve a considerable amount of paperwork.

A further problem arises with respect to debt. Just as interest income is mismeasured during inflation, so is interest expense. Debtors benefit when inflation depreciates the real value of their outstanding debts. So if bond-holders may report negative income for inflation's depreciation of their assets, debtors will have to claim positive income for inflation's depreciation of their debts. There is no way that the effect of inflation on debtors can be ignored if assets are indexed. Without indexation of debt, taxpayers would be able to borrow and lend, deduct nominal interest expense but include only real interest income, and shelter all their income from tax.

Taxpayers, particularly homeowners with mortgages, may find the increased taxes on debt a rude shock; there seems to be a popular sense that indexation would result only in tax cuts, not in some tax increases. Another possible misconception is that indexation would be added to the preferences already in the law. Allowing indexation of capital gains on top of the capital gains exclusion would involve a substantial revenue loss. To maintain revenues, indexing capital gains would have to replace the exclusion, not supplement it. Similarly, the budget could not afford indexing the historical cost of business machines and buildings and then depreciating that cost under the rapid ACRS schedules. Indexation of depreciation allowances would certainly require a slowing of ACRS. Businesses might find accelerated unindexed allowances more attractive than low stated allowances that would increase with inflation.

Another aspect of indexation is its effect on taxpayer uncertainty. An indexed tax base would fix the outcomes of all borrowing and lending transactions in real dollars, and these are the terms in which economists think. Businesses deal in nominal dollars, however. If the tax bases were indexed, a business that knew in advance and with certainty its net income in nominal dollars would not know its tax liability in nominal dollars, because that would depend on the inflation rate. So indexation might decrease uncertainty in theory, but it would probably increase uncertainty in practice. Moreover, the inflation rate, and thus the factor for indexing income from capital and interest expense, would not be known until after the tax year was over; as a result, the tax filing process would be delayed.

Finally, there are risks of perpetuating inflation and amplifying inflationary shocks if the economy becomes more fully indexed. If all transactions were indexed, a price increase in one sector would be transmitted quickly throughout the economy. The economy is not completely indexed, and indexing the tax base will not make it so; but the more complete the indexation, the less the friction against inflationary shocks in the economy (though also, admittedly, the less the pain of inflation).

With these drawbacks, should a restructured income tax index the tax base? Here are some other points to be considered:

First, inflation has remained low since 1982. The costs of indexation in terms of complexity and tax administration, not to mention risks of perpetuating inflation, are considerable; the lower the costs of inflation—in part, the lower the inflation rate—the less attractive is indexation. But, if inflation should accelerate, an unindexed income tax would induce distortions.

Second, the lower the marginal tax rates, the lower the overtaxation from inflation-induced distortions. If restructuring the income tax allows substantial reductions of marginal tax rates, indexation will become that much less necessary.

Third, interest rates adjust for inflation, and to some extent that adjustment makes indexation less necessary. There was certainly an allowance for anticipated or feared inflation in 14 percent mortgages written in recent years while inflation was 4 or 5 percent; if the interest rate were indexed (or if the tax base were indexed) there is little doubt that the stated interest rate would be different. (Of course, this suggests that tax indexation of interest income and expense should be restricted to contracts written after the effective date of indexing. If borrowers and lenders agreed to an interest rate in anticipation of inflation and income tax effects, it would be unfair to change the definition of taxable interest income and expense at that same interest rate.)

The market adjustment of interest rates for inflation can hold precisely unchanged the after-tax income of a borrower and a lender if they are in the same tax-rate bracket.[6] Thus, under restrictive conditions, inflation has no distorting effect on after-tax incomes (though it does cause mismeasurement of taxable income). Although these conditions would rarely hold in practice, restructuring the income tax would reduce the maximum gap between the marginal tax rates of borrower and lender (equal to the difference between the highest rate and zero). Thus, with no specific provision for inflation, restructuring the income tax would reduce distortions caused by inflation.

The United States has hesitated to index its tax base because of the complexity and other costs of doing so. At low rates of inflation, indexation is less necessary; the benefits of a restructured income tax would make indexing less needed still.

---

6. Vito Tanzi, *Inflation and the Personal Income Tax: An International Perspective* (Cambridge, England: Cambridge University Press, 1980), Chapters 10 and 11.

The Corporate Income Tax

Under the U.S. income tax, income from unincorporated businesses (sole proprietorships or partnerships) is taxed only on the individual income tax returns of their owners, while income of corporations is taxed under a separate corporate income tax. When corporate income is distributed to the shareholders, they pay tax on it as well. Part of the debate over restructuring the income tax concerns whether we should have a separate corporate income tax.

Why a Corporate Income Tax?

The basic rationale for a separate corporate income tax is to protect the individual income tax. If the corporate tax were repealed but nothing else changed, corporations could be manipulated to avoid individual taxes. Individuals could transfer their wealth to specially formed corporations; the money could be invested to earn interest (or other forms of investment income), which would not be taxable until the corporations redistributed it in the form of dividends. Individuals would profit, and government revenues would suffer, from this deferral of individual income tax liability.

The problem is that when corporate income is distributed after being taxed at the corporate level, it is taxed again at the shareholder's level. This "double taxation of dividends" discriminates against large businesses that require the benefits of incorporation (principally limited liability, the ability to retain earnings, and a potentially unlimited number of owners) and against others. Investment capital is thus diverted away from the corporate sector. (Since 1958, corporations that have some maximum number of owners— thirty-five—and meet certain other requirements can have the best of both worlds by choosing the so-called Subchapter S status and being taxed as partnerships. Despite this advantage, some corporations that would qualify have not chosen Subchapter S status, and therefore have paid the corporate tax.)

Some critics go so far as to argue that no corporate tax is justified. For this viewpoint, income accrues to the benefit of individuals only when they receive and consume it. This school of thought supports expenditure taxation rather than income taxation.

The separate corporate tax is defended against this charge on other grounds. The status of corporations as legal persons is seen as fitting reason for separate taxation. The costs that corporations impose on society (such as congestion and pollution) and their power as institutions are also cited. These arguments unquestionably have strong popular appeal, and there is an overwhelming consensus in favor of the corporate tax. Nonetheless, such arguments do not refute the charge of misallocation of investment between the incorporated and unincorporated business sectors.

The next line of defense for the corporate tax is the deficit. Despite its undesirable side effects, the corporate tax raises revenue. With large budget deficits, any revenue lost by modifying or eliminating the corporate tax would have to be replaced by some other means. When added to a necessary net tax increase, this additional burden could impose considerable pain and cause distortions elsewhere in the economy.

Finally, despite the interest and discussion among economists and business leaders over the years, there is still no workable, nondivisive way to eliminate the corporate tax. Because of its function of protecting the individual income tax, the corporation income tax cannot just be repealed; safeguards would be needed to keep corporations from becoming potential tax shelters.

The required approach is called integration of the corporate and individual income taxes.[7] Under integration, shareholders would pay tax on all corporate net income every year, whether it was distributed or retained. Each corporation would notify all shareholders of their pro rata share of the firm's profits each year. A corporate tax would be levied, but only as a withholding device; all tax so collected would be attributed to shareholders as tax credits, just as withholding on wages or salaries is credited. Thus, under integration, all corporate income would be taxed at the tax rates applicable to shareholders, not at a separate rate attributable to corporations, and all corporate income would be taxed only once.

Whatever its theoretical advantages, integration would involve monumental practical problems. For one thing, large corporations' tax returns are invariably audited and typically are not final for several years. Furthermore, many corporations use fiscal years different from the calendar year. There would be problems attributing corporate income among shares that were sold (perhaps several times) during the year. All this would make timely attribution of corporate income to individuals extremely difficult.[8] Still further problems arise in the handling of corporations that show tax losses (39 percent did in 1980)[9] because of the potential for trafficking in such losses as tax deductions

---

7. Charles McLure, *Must Corporate Income Be Taxed Twice?* (Washington, D.C.: The Brookings Institution, 1979) explains the issues and options in detail.

8. The practical solution might be to make current shareholders responsible for the tax consequences of any audit adjustments, even if they did not own shares in the year for which the corporation's return is being audited.

9. U.S. Department of the Treasury, Internal Revenue Service, *Statistics of Income—1980, Corporation Income Tax Returns* (Washington, D.C.: U.S. Government Printing Office, 1983), table 17, p. 67.

among shareholders. (That is, high-bracket taxpayers could buy shares of loss corporations from low-bracket individuals or nontaxable institutions merely to deduct the losses on their tax returns.) Foreign-source income of corporations would pose problems, as would treatment of foreign, nontaxable and nonprofit shareholders of U.S. corporations. Integration would reduce tax revenue, which would force tax rates up. Finally, corporations would have to pay withholding tax at the highest individual rate (so that taxpayers would not have to come up with cash from other sources to pay tax on their attributed share of the corporation's income that was not distributed in cash), which would reduce many corporations' customary levels of retained earnings; this would displease corporate managers. In short, implementing integration would be extraordinarily difficult, and despite integration's reduction of business taxes, many business interests (primarily corporate managers) would not like the drain on retained earnings.

A less ambitious step would be to leave the corporate tax in place but merely to eliminate the double taxation of dividends; this course is sometimes referred to as "dividend relief." Dividend relief would be much simpler than integration, but still would have problems of its own. Merely making dividends deductible at the corporate level would cost considerable tax revenue. Giving individual taxpayers a credit for corporate taxes paid on dividends raises some of the problems of integration, including primarily the delay in determining actual corporate taxes paid and the treatment of foreign taxes and tax losses.[10] Furthermore, in contrast to the neutrality of full integration with respect to dividend payouts (all corporate income would be taxed only once, at the marginal rate of the shareholder), dividend relief would provide a positive inducement to pay dividends (corporate retentions would be taxed at the corporate rate, which is higher than the rate of many shareholders, and any subsequent capital gain would be taxed still further).

Economists tend to favor greater payouts (because retained earnings can be reinvested, even though more profitable uses for the funds could be available outside the corporation that earned them). But corporate managers would not want the resultant pressure from shareholders to pay more dividends. A Carter administration dividend relief plan that was leaked to the press in 1977 proved highly controversial for these reasons and was never actually proposed.[11]

---

10. These problems would be mitigated to some degree if corporate tax preferences were largely repealed and tax were based on net income more accurately defined.

11. "Tax Reform Option Papers Prepared by Treasury Department, September 2, 1977, for the White House," Bureau of National Affairs, *Daily Report for Executives*, Special Supplement DER 196 (October 7, 1977).

For all the problems, there is no consensus on what to do about the corporate income tax. With the administrative problems of integration and the need for revenue, there is little prospect of eliminating the corporate tax, and even dividend relief would be difficult to attain.

Depreciation and the Investment Tax Credit

As was noted in the preceding chapter, the personal expenditure tax would eliminate the need for gradual tax depreciation by substituting complete expensing in the year an investment was made. In the absence of this simple and completely neutral (albeit at a zero effective rate of tax) solution through a personal expenditure tax, depreciation must be allowed over the useful lives of assets under the income tax.[12]

The ACRS is far more generous than true economic depreciation (that is, the rate at which assets actually lose their value), and ACRS is not even-handed in its treatment of different investments. The shortest-lived assets (primarily automobiles) are written off over three years; the treatment of these assets was so generous that abuse had to be corrected in the Deficit Reduction Act of 1984.[13] ACRS lumps virtually all other equipment into a second category, depreciated at an accelerated rate over five years; so the longest-lived assets in that category are treated more generously than the shortest. Finally, structures were depreciated over fifteen years in the original legislation; rapidly growing tax shelter activity, plus the need for revenue, led to a lengthening of building depreciation lives to eighteen years in the 1984 law.

ACRS was made generous in part to stimulate investment. Rapid tax depreciation and an up-front investment tax credit score well under the standard economic model of investment behavior, known as the cost-of-capital model. This approach measures the total cost to the user of the services of a unit of capital—in this context, with particular emphasis on the role of taxation. All else being equal, if tax benefits for investment increase, the cost

---

12. Immediate expensing is difficult to incorporate into an income tax system, because expensing and the deductibility of interest on borrowing to finance investments in physical capital are generally held to be excessive tax benefits. But deductibility of mortgage interest is probably a sacrosanct feature of the tax law, and deductibility of interest on business loans to buy assets other than those subject to expensing would still be proper. Thus, expensing under an income tax would require allowing interest deductions for loans for some purposes but not for others; but because of the fungibility of money (that is, money from borrowing and from other sources can be intermingled, with no way to know which money is used for one of several purposes), such selective disallowances of interest deductions would be extremely difficult if not possible.

13. Business automobiles could be depreciated over three years with a 6 percent investment credit, resulting in alleged abusive overinvestment in luxury automobiles for business purposes.

of capital will go down and firms will invest more. In the long run, assuming full employment, this investment will substitute capital for labor. In the recent past, with the economy below full employment, the desired effect of ACRS was to encourage firms to expand and replace obsolete plant and equipment more rapidly than they would otherwise.

Ironically, this approach to stimulating investment works best when marginal tax rates are high. If a firm faces a high tax rate on its profit, any tax deduction is correspondingly valuable. Thus, a high corporate or individual tax rate, coupled with generous depreciation allowances (and an investment tax credit), can induce a corporation or an unincorporated business to reinvest a larger share of its net income, thereby reducing taxable income and taxes. In effect, the federal government pays the business to invest more.

This approach has its benefits. The large subsidies through the investment tax credit and accelerated depreciation encourage new investment. At the same time, after the subsidies are claimed, the high tax rate rakes in a large share of any remaining profit. Thus, the high-tax-rate and high-subsidy strategy is generous to new investment, and so encourages it, but is much more rigorous toward old investment and any extraordinary profit. This distinction between old and new capital is taken to be an advantage.

The high-tax-rate and high-subsidy policy has some disadvantages as well, however; its case is hardly open and shut. In general, both the high tax rates and the high subsidies cause problems of their own.

First, the current law's approach, for all its implicit emphasis on new investment and innovation, is biased against firms that are new and firms that are turning the corner from recent losses. ACRS is accelerated in that it gives deductions in the early years that are greater than the income typically generated by investments; the ITC amplifies this acceleration. If a firm has no other income and tax liability from which to deduct these tax benefits and so cannot use them immediately, it must wait until some time in the future, making the benefits correspondingly less valuable. Thus, new firms and rebuilding firms get much less from ACRS than do established, profitable firms. Accumulations of unused depreciation allowances and investment tax credits in some firms have fueled the boom in corporate mergers—another instance of the influence of the tax law on economic choices that would be best left to the market.

This bias of the high-subsidy approach was foreseen when ACRS was passed; the proposed solution was the safe-harbor tax-leasing provision of the 1981 law. Under safe-harbor leasing, a firm that could not use the tax deductions or credits from an investment could sell the asset to another firm in a paper transaction. The nominal owner could use the tax benefits, and then lease the asset back to the actual user. The rent would be set low, so that in effect the nominal user and the owner split the tax benefits. Thus, in the final analysis, the nominal owner helped the user to cash in the tax benefits, in exchange for a percentage of the action.

The problem with safe-harbor leasing was largely appearances. The public reacted strongly against what it perceived as the buying and selling of tax breaks. The resentment centered on subsidies going to "losers," and on large, profitable firms seemingly buying their way out of their tax obligations (some profitable firms used safe-harbor leasing to pay no tax at all).[14] Political reality forced repeal of safe-harbor leasing, and its replacement by a system under which unprofitable users of investment assets are expected to get a smaller share of their own tax benefits. Most economists would probably disagree with this popular verdict; there seems to be little justification for restricting an intended investment subsidy to established, profitable firms. But if insuperable political constraints prevent the high-tax-rate and high-subsidy approach from functioning properly, that real world weakness of the whole approach cannot be ignored.

A second weakness of the high-subsidy approach is its unfavorable treatment of firms in certain industries, particularly the so-called high-technology sector. Depreciable physical capital—plant and equipment—is only one form of investment. Firms also invest in inventories, land, knowledge, and other assets. Although the tax treatment of nondepreciable assets varies with their exact nature, high tax rates can put such investments at a disadvantage in comparison with heavily subsidized depreciable assets. Thus, although the current system has the perhaps desirable effect of taxing old depreciable capital heavily, it can tax *all nondepreciable* capital heavily as well. This is another instance of intrusion of the tax law into market decisions.

There is evidence that the current tax system is especially hard on the high-technology sector[15]—ironic, considering the ostensible emphasis of the tax law on growth. One reason is that high-technology firms make less intensive use of depreciable capital, and more intensive use of knowledge, than many others; ACRS and the ITC are of little help for firms with that asset mix. Another reason is that high-technology firms tend to be new and small, and thus unable to make immediate use of large tax subsidies. A final reason is that technologically advanced activities tend to be economically risky, with

---

14. Joint Committee on Taxation, *Analysis of Safe-Harbor Leasing* (Washington, D.C.: U.S. Government Printing Office, June 14, 1982), p. 22; Scott R. Schmedel, "GE's Huge Tax-Leasing Benefits Expected to Heighten Controversy over 1981 Law," *Wall Street Journal*, March 15, 1982, p. 8.

15. Charles R. Hulten and James W. Robertson, "The Taxation of High Technology Industries," *The National Tax Journal*, vol. 37 (September 1984), pp. 327-45.

a low probability of profit but a high payoff if they succeed. Under the current tax approach, those high payoffs are subjected to high statutory tax rates.

This suggests that the current law is more favorable to conservative, low-return investments than it is to more risky, high-return ones. The generous tax benefits can make an investment with a low expected return look more attractive than it would be otherwise. Conversely, an investment that might have a big payoff would have to face a high statutory tax rate, making the risk look less attractive. Of course, an alternative would be to move the investment to some other country where statutory rates are lower.

Again, the 1981 law had a proposed remedy for an anticipated problem. In this case, it was the tax credit for incremental research and development (R&D) expenditures. This credit equals 25 percent of R&D expenditures in excess of the firm's average for the preceding three years, and the provision is scheduled to expire at the end of 1985. The intent was to give knowledge-intensive firms a subsidy to balance the ACRS subsidy for capital-intensive firms. The R&D credit has serious flaws as an incentive, however: it offers little if any benefit to ongoing R&D programs at a constant level of effort; it is of limited help to new firms; it wastes federal revenues on activities that are classified as R&D only for purposes of claiming the credit; and it is somewhat self-defeating, in that R&D subsidized in one year increases the three-year average for future years and thus discourages R&D later. Enhancing the incentive would add considerably to the revenue cost of the credit. So there are no easy remedies to the bias of the high-tax-rate and high-subsidy approach toward particular kinds of firms.

This bias of the current law toward conservative investments has a predictable side effect of encouraging tax shelters. ACRS, the ITC, and other tax subsidies are large enough that people who know the law can combine them in investments that make money after taxes, though they make little or no money before taxes. As was noted earlier, investments in tax shelters have boomed since ACRS was enacted. Thus, the current tax system encourages economic waste.

The high-tax-rate and high-subsidy approach would be hard to perpetuate under a restructured income tax. There is widespread agreement on the importance of bringing individual income tax rates down. If that happens, sole proprietorships and partnerships will be less influenced by tax deductions (such as those under ACRS), because deductions will have less value. Of course, to reduce tax rates at no revenue cost or even a gain, many preferences (including those for investment) must be repealed or reduced anyway. If those preferences were repealed for individuals but not for corporations, or if tax rates were substantially different between the two taxes, there would be distortions and opportunities for manipulation. So if we want low tax rates and low or no subsidies under the individual income tax, the corporate tax likely will probably have to go along for the ride. Given the current revenues, amounts of tax expenditures, and tax rates charged under the two taxes, restructuring along similar lines could result in coordinated, lower tax rates with revenues higher than those under the current law.

Reducing corporate tax rates would have the undesirable effect of lowering taxes on existing depreciable capital investments, thus conferring a windfall. This windfall would be a one-time-only transfer, and once the existing capital wore out, the income it had generated would have to be reinvested under the new rules. A remedy for these windfalls would be to phase in the rate reductions, but care would be needed to avoid building incentives for postponement of investment and receipt of income, and opportunities for manipulation, into the law. Of course, to the extent that current high rates disproportionately burden *nondepreciable* investments today, the rate cut is called for immediately to alleviate that excessive burden.

Conclusion

The corporate income tax is probably a necessary element of our current tax system because of revenue needs and administrative issues, even though many experts argue that it has no theoretical role to play. If the individual income tax were restructured, with fewer preferences and lower rates, the corporate tax probably would be similarly modified.

Summary

The current income tax system has important shortcomings, but a major advantage of staying within the framework of the income tax system, despite its faults, is continuity. Though individual provisions of a restructured income tax may involve transition problems of their own, there would be no change in the fundamental definition of the tax base. But within its basic framework, a restructured income tax could make focused improvements in fairness, simplicity, and economic efficiency.

Any major tax change would involve potentially painful adjustments on the part of taxpayers and some reshuffling of the tax burden. Taxpayers who stand to lose from such a change can be expected to defend their interests, and the political process will feel their influence. Would the benefits of such a restructuring outweigh the real costs of change? Could the political system manage such a significant step? Would income tax reform help to reduce the deficit, or will we attack the deficit in some less radical way, or perhaps not attack the deficit at all? We face unprecedented political pressures arising from equally unprecedented economic forces. The resolution will depend on politics as well as economics.

CHAPTER 7

MAKING A CHOICE

Tax policymakers clearly have many tasks in the second half of the 1980s. In coordination with spending cuts and overall fiscal policy, the tax system must help to close the deficit gap. The tax system must interfere as little as possible with efficient allocation of all resources in every sector of the economy. The tax burden must be distributed fairly among households and businesses, closely enough to the historical pattern that painful adjustments are kept to a minimum. And the tax system must be simple enough in its broad outline, and burdened with few enough detailed exceptions, that most people can understand and trust it.

The list of criteria is sufficiently long that no one policy option can fully satisfy them all. All the alternatives discussed in the preceding chapters have both advantages and disadvantages. The best policy choice is the one that achieves the best balance among all the criteria.

One of the main criteria for a tax policy is political acceptability; whatever its advantages, a tax alternative that cannot become law is of little use. Given that political and economic circumstances are extraordinary, however, there is no way to know with certainty what political acceptability is. Any statement on tax politics now is no more than a forecast and an assertion.

The public interest must coexist with political reality on several fronts. Nonetheless, we should buy all the economic benefit that our tax politics can afford. In the remainder of this chapter, we put our economic interests in a political context, first by examining the economic imperatives of tax policy in a period of large budget deficits, and then by considering how we might make that economic medicine as palatable as possible. This is no guarantee of success, only an opportunity. Whatever the political unknowns, we must face up to the tax issue; there is no escaping it.

Economic Essentials

The analysis in the preceding chapters indicates that either the value-added tax or an increase in rates under the existing income tax is attractive only as a last resort. The value-added tax would require a new bureaucracy and more paperwork, would burden poor and near-poor households, and would require still further paperwork to reduce that burden. An increase in the income tax rates would increase disincentives and distortions in the current system and would add to the burden of taxpayers who already pay too much. In short, although these options are preferable to continued megadeficits, neither is terribly attractive.

The only options that address the problems of the existing income tax as well as the deficit are the personal expenditure tax and the restructured income tax. Of the two, the personal expenditure tax may have the greater theoretical appeal, but it also has enormous practical problems. Transition to a personal expenditure tax would be a long and painful process. Tax administration and compliance would be complicated by the necessary additional reporting of saving and borrowing. Revenue would be lost through deductions that would be needed for taxpayers who had saved in the past out of fully taxed income. When these problems are added to the tax's appearance of unfairness through the shifting of the tax burden toward the young, the old, and borrowers, it becomes apparent that the personal expenditure tax carries excess baggage as a timely deficit remedy and tax reform.

In contrast to establishing a personal expenditure tax, restructuring the income tax system is a much more modest exercise. Rather than converting the entire tax base, income tax restructuring zeroes in on problem areas in the existing base. Major problems can be eased, while no new systemwide transition problems are imposed. From this perspective, the income tax seems to be the better choice—it allows quicker action on the deficit, and its effects are more certain.

There remains the question of where to get the additional tax revenue. Because simple increases in the tax rates cause problems rather than solving them, the only course remaining is to repeal income tax preferences. In this regard it makes no difference whether we choose a restructured income tax or a personal expenditure tax; the job is the same. Actually, because the personal expenditure tax has a smaller tax base (all else being equal) and involves a transitional revenue loss, it requires even more broadening of the tax base (or higher rates) than the income tax.

The 1982 and 1984 deficit reduction laws made some progress toward repealing income tax preferences, but they did not go nearly far enough to be a long-term remedy, and members of Congress have described these laws as extremely difficult to pass. A new bill that repealed more tax preferences than the earlier laws, approaching fundamental tax restructuring, might or might not be even more painful. A fundamental restructuring would touch many more interest groups than the recent laws did, but those groups that were touched would not be so much singled out. In addition, if the restructuring went far enough, all affected groups could at least have a tax rate reduction as partial compensation. So despite the pain of the tax legislative process in 1982 and 1984, further progress should not be written off. In this section, we discuss how the essential parts of a restructured income tax—a broadened tax base, relief for low-income persons, and reduced tax rates—would work.

If tax reform is to reduce the deficit and tax rates as well, the base broadening must touch some of the most entrenched provisions in the income tax law. If we fail to achieve action on most of these major tax preferences, deficit reduction can only fall back to several more rounds of "cats and dogs" legislation, simple rate increases, or a value-added tax. To give some sense of what will be in store, this discussion covers the largest items in the tax expenditure list.

We chose the tax preferences discussed in this section largely because of the size of the revenue loss they cause. This list does not exhaust the list of preferences that could be repealed or cut back on tax policy grounds; in fact, many more must be tackled if the tax base is to be sufficiently broadened.

The Tax Base

Homeowner Deductions. The so-called homeowner deductions—for home mortgage interest and local real property taxes—are in one sense the most basic itemized deductions under the individual income tax. The home mortgage interest deduction is what puts many middle-income households over the line from claiming the standard deduction to itemizing their deductions. The property tax deduction reinforces the mortgage interest deduction in making many homeowners itemize. In 1982, almost half of all itemizers fell in the $25,000 to $50,000 income range, and they claimed more than 40 percent of their deductions for mortgage interest and property taxes.[1] The revenue cost of these two provisions is considerable—$25 billion for the

1. U.S. Department of the Treasury, Internal Revenue Service, *Statistics of Income—1982 Individual Income Tax Returns* (Washington, D.C.: U.S. Government Printing Office, 1984), table 2.1, p. 60–61.

mortgage interest deduction and $10 billion for the property tax deduction in fiscal 1985, according to the tax expenditure list.[2]

The tax treatment of homeownership is not "correct" by the standards of some tax experts. According to this viewpoint, interest expense is properly deductible only when it is a cost of earning income.[3] Mortgage interest is paid to finance the purchase of an asset, the owner-occupied home, which generates "income" (in the form of the services that the home provides) that is not subject to tax. (Consider the situation of the owner of a house who rents it out. The owner pays tax on the rental income received, less deductions for all legitimate expenses, such as interest on a business loan and depreciation and repairs on the house. Proper tax treatment does not change if the owner implicitly rents the house to himself; he should pay tax on the implicit rental value, net of his expenses of interest, depreciation, and repairs. Thus, the deduction for mortgage interest is a deduction for part of the expense, even though there is no tax on the income.) The property tax deduction might also be questioned on the ground that the property tax is a price paid for local services; the more the taxes paid in a particular locality (all else being equal), the more government services are rendered, and so a deduction for what is in effect a payment for services would not be appropriate. The property tax deduction is also sometimes challenged as an inordinate benefit to homeowners relative to renters, who may implicitly pay property tax as part of their rent.

The rationale for the mortgage interest and property tax deductions is twofold. First, these deductions are seen as incentives to homeownership, which is believed to increase attachment to the community and responsibility. Second, the deduction is thought to help young and moderate-income families to afford homes. These are nonmarket goals of the type that cannot be left to the unguided workings of the economy.

The counterargument is that these tax deductions do not achieve their goals. The deductions may simply raise the price of land and existing homes, conferring windfalls on owners and not encouraging homeownership. Moreover, the deductions may be poor subsidies to struggling first-time home buyers, because the deductions are worth the most to taxpayers with the most income (therefore in the highest tax brackets); by this standard, it is not the marginal home buyers but the better-off who benefit most from the deductions.

---

2. Joint Committee on Taxation, *Estimates of Federal Tax Expenditures for Fiscal Years 1984–1989* (Washington, D.C.: U.S. Government Printing Office, November 9, 1984), table 1, pp. 9–16.

3. Richard Goode, *The Individual Income Tax* (Washington, D.C.: The Brookings Institution, 1976), pp. 148–53.

For the well-to-do, these deductions can subsidize not starter homes but luxury and vacation homes.

Finally, some economists argue that if homeownership is encouraged, investment is diverted from business capital that would add to productive capacity. We would be better off in the long run, from this point of view, if investment were not diverted into residential capital.

Despite all the problems with the homeowner deductions, they would be virtually impossible to repeal. Beyond their sheer popularity, they have become embedded in the economy. Millions of taxpayers have bought homes and taken out long-term mortgages. Repealing the mortgage interest deduction would not only increase taxes for those families, it would also decrease the market value of their homes. Thus, if the tax increases were more than taxpayers' budgets could handle (a situation that would principally afflict persons who bought homes recently and paid inflated prices at high interest rates), these homeowners would not have the normal escape of selling their homes, because such sales would leave them with large capital losses. Mortgage lenders would be at risk on their loans on these properties. Home builders would be threatened because reduced demand for their products would be felt in a temporary slowdown of new construction.

The long term of the mortgage contract and the high proportion of families' net worth in their homes distinguish the homeowner deductions from others. Repeal of these deductions is accordingly difficult. Tax restructuring will probably have to yield to this political and economic reality. The best that can be attained may be some limit on excesses. In theory, limiting the deductions to primary residences would be fairer and would yield more revenue. In practice, the amount of revenue gained by limiting the deduction to one home per taxpayer would be small and would drop even further as wealthy homeowners consolidated their mortgages from multiple homes into large single mortgages on their primary homes. The gain in fairness would be small for the same reason.

Another approach would be to limit the amount of the mortgage interest deduction to some maximum amount, which would limit the subsidy to relatively basic housing or to fractions of the cost of luxury homes. This approach has the weakness that the deduction limit would be contentious. If it were set high enough to affect few taxpayers, it would raise little revenue; but if set lower, it would affect more taxpayers with homes of near-average value. The limit could be set relatively high to start, but be held fixed in nominal dollars so that inflation would increase its effect over time. Even so, there could be fairness problems.

The amount of mortgage interest paid is a function of the size of the mortgage and the interest rate. People who bought their homes recently paid high prices, borrowed at high interest rates, and have paid off little of the balance of their mortgages. In contrast, people who have been in their homes for a decade or more borrowed at rates much below the current level, have smaller outstanding balances, and have profited from market appreciation. Thus, a $100,000 home—about the national average—with an 80 percent mortgage at a 14 percent interest rate requires $11,200 of mortgage interest to be paid in the first year. If the amount of mortgage interest that could be deducted annually were capped at $10,000, only about $2.6 billion per year would be raised by fiscal 1989,[4] but obviously people who recently bought homes of average value would be hurt. For perspective, though, the average millionaire itemizer of mortgage interest in 1982 paid only about $18,000 of mortgage interest, because millionaires are typically older and have lived in their homes for longer periods, and thus have smaller mortgages relative to their homes' values with lower interest rates. In fact, less than half of all millionaires itemized any mortgage interest at all; the others own their homes outright or rent.[5] Thus, most millionaires would not be affected by a mortgage interest deduction cap, but many middle-income taxpayers who bought their homes recently would be.

A third option would be to convert the mortgage interest deduction to a credit, rather than allowing the deduction to be worth more to high-bracket than to lower-bracket taxpayers.[6] This approach has the advantage of giving well-to-do taxpayers no more benefit than first-time homebuyers, who need the subsidy most. The disadvantage is administrative. Interest as a cost of earning income (as in the case of a loan for business equipment or a margin loan for an investor) is properly deductible from the income that it generates, and at the same marginal tax rate. Owners of businesses or investors who in effect borrow against their homes to raise capital should be allowed to deduct their mortgage interest at the same tax rate as the rate that is charged on their business or investment income. Thus, mortgage interest would have to be deductible at the highest applicable marginal rate if the taxpayers had investment income. This would be slightly complex, and although it would be

---

4. Congressional Budget Office, *Reducing the Deficit: Spending and Revenue Options* (Washington, D.C.: U.S. Government Printing Office, February 1984), p. 199. This assumes that no other features of the current law were changed.

5. U.S. Department of the Treasury, Internal Revenue Service, *Statistics of Income—1982 Individual Income Tax Returns* (Washington, D.C.: U.S. Government Printing Office, 1984), table 2.1, pp. 60–61. This pattern holds true across the upper-income brackets. About two-thirds of all taxpayers with incomes between $100,000 and $200,000 itemize mortgage interest, for example, with the average amount less than $8,000.

6. This is an approach applied to all deductions (in different ways) by the Bradley-Gephardt Fair Tax Act and the Hatfield Simpliform Tax Act.

perfectly proper, it could appear to favor homeowners with other wealth over those without.

Any change in homeowner deductions could be grandfathered in—that is, applied only to future homebuyers—but this practice would not eliminate the impact on current owners. They would face no immediate change in their tax deductions, but their homes would still depreciate in market value because any prospective buyer would obtain less tax benefit. Thus, grandfathering as a transition device has strictly limited value.

So the homeowner deductions would be difficult to repeal or to cut back significantly, even though such action would be good tax policy in the abstract. These political contraints cannot be ignored. Perhaps the best approach would be to limit the deductions in one of the ways described here, even though the revenue gain would be small. Of course, if homeowner deductions are treated relatively leniently, other tax preferences must be treated that much more rigorously to reduce the deficit and fund tax rate reductions.

Even if retaining homeowner deductions in a restructured income tax is unavoidable, the tax system and the economy would still be better off. In the long run, reducing tax rates through restructuring would improve economic efficiency and equity with respect to owner-occupied housing as well as in other respects. Reducing rates would modestly reduce the incentive to invest in owner-occupied housing and would notably reduce the subsidy to luxury housing (to the extent that the highest tax rates were reduced).

Other Itemized Deductions. Itemized deductions other than those for homeowners would have to be cut back to restructure the income tax.

The deduction for *medical expenses* was intended to compensate taxpayers who had large and unavoidable medical care costs. As was noted earlier, the medical cost deduction became overly complex and was simplified and cut back by the 1982 deficit reduction tax bill. The expected fiscal 1985 revenue cost of the deduction, after the 1982 cutback, is about $3 billion.[7]

Still further action may be justified. The current law allows medical expenses in excess of 5 percent of income to be deducted. Given the level of medical care costs in the economy today, 5 percent of income might be seen as a relatively typical level; 10 percent might be a more fitting cutoff for extraordinary costs. Another structural issue, mentioned earlier, is whether capital improvements on a taxpayer's home, vacations, or like expenditures should be considered medical care costs under any circumstances.

---

7. Joint Committee on Taxation, *Estimates of Federal Tax Expenditures*, table 1, pp. 9–16.

Consumer interest deductions are allowed in part to stimulate sales of consumer goods, especially automobiles and other durables; these deductions will reduce revenues by about $7 billion in fiscal 1985.[8] The deductions have the same flaw as the deduction for mortgage interest, in that interest is deductible even though it is not a cost of earning taxable income. But the consumer interest deduction has the same defense as the mortgage interest deduction, in that business owners and investors can finance their investments by carrying consumer loans. Thus, outright repeal of the consumer interest deduction would not be proper; a more correct (but unfortunately more complicated) step would be to allow interest to be deducted, but only to the extent of business or investment income.

Taxpayers may deduct *state and local taxes* because taxes are considered mandatory expenditures that yield no specific benefit. Without a deduction, some would argue, the federal income tax would be "a tax on a tax." (This effect is strongest for taxpayers subject to the highest marginal rates under the federal, state, and sometimes local income taxes.) Most experts see the deduction as a subsidy to states and localities, but it is so only in that federal income tax itemizers receive some relief for their state and local taxes. The deduction reduces the tax burden more in states with high taxes, thereby equalizing the burden across states somewhat. Deductibility of state and local taxes (other than real property taxes) will reduce federal revenues by about $27 billion in fiscal 1985.[9]

The sales and personal property tax deductions can be challenged on the ground that these taxes are relatively small and predictable expenses, which might be adequately compensated through the personal exemptions and zero-bracket amounts. Furthermore, counting precise sales tax payments is extremely tedious, so many taxpayers use inexact tables provided by the IRS. Repeal of deductions for personal property taxes and sales taxes would be attractive on federal tax policy grounds.

States and localities might oppose such repeals because they would interfere with the choice of state and local tax instruments; a state or local government would prefer to increase a deductible rather than a nondeductible tax, all else being equal. The state and local revenue arsenal is already so influenced, however, in that gasoline taxes and user charges are not deductible. Some thought has been given to complete repeal of deductibility, which would leave states and localities completely unfettered in their choices of tax

8. Ibid.
9. Ibid.

instruments, with compensation in the form of increased federal grants.[10] The difficulty would be agreeing on a formula for dividing the grants among the states and localities, as in every other federal grant program. The November 1984 Treasury tax proposals would repeal all state and local tax deductions but make no provision for additional federal grants.

Charitable contributions are deductible mainly as an incentive. If the cost of giving is reduced by a tax deduction, people may give more. When people make tax-deductible gifts to charity, their cost is less than the amount they hand over by the amount of their tax saving; the federal government makes up the difference through an implicit matching grant. These matching grants are expected to total $15 billion in fiscal 1985.[11] Without that incentive, many worthwhile causes might be left to the federal government for support. It would be extremely difficult for government to choose which causes to support. Through the deduction, taxpayers implicitly make those choices for the government; the government gives its matching grants to the causes that the people support. This incentive has been broadened by a provision of the 1981 law allowing limited deductions for nonitemizers in addition to their standard deductions. This provision expires at the end of 1986.

The charitable contribution deduction enjoys wide general support. The only blanket indictment would be that it favors causes supported by upper-income people, because their higher tax rates make their cost of giving lower (in other words, the government's matching grants are larger). The additional deduction for nonitemizers is sometimes opposed on three grounds: (1) as a complication of the law for the people whose tax returns most need to be simple; (2) as an unnecessary additional benefit, because the standard deduction is intended to replace itemized deductions; and (3) as an unfortunate precedent for possible additional complicating deductions for nonitemizers. Perhaps the most vehement opposition is to the deduction for gifts of appreciated property, measured at their current value rather than at their original cost. Under this provision, for example, someone who bought stock for $10 that is now worth $100 could give it to a charitable organization and claim a $100 deduction. The resulting tax saving is much larger than it would be if the taxpayer realized the $90 capital gain and then gave $100 in cash. This

---

10. Nonna A. Noto and Dennis Zimmerman, "Limiting State-Local Tax Deductibility in Exchange for Increased General Revenue Sharing: An Analysis of the Economic Effects," Library of Congress, Congressional Research Service, June 2, 1983, processed.

11. Joint Committee on Taxation, *Estimates of Federal Tax Expenditures*, table 1, pp. 9–16.

deduction is even more unpopular after widely publicized instances of donors' overstating the value of gifts of property to obtain greater tax savings.[12]

The deduction for charitable contributions illustrates one alleged weakness of the restructured income tax. In general, if tax rates are reduced, any tax incentives in the form of deductions or exclusions become less powerful. (To people who want to reduce the intrusion of the tax law into private decision making, this weakness is really a strength.) In the case of the deduction for charitable contributions, the cost of giving each dollar to charity increases if marginal tax rates are reduced, even if no change is made in the deduction itself. The reason is that the federal government's implicit matching grants are reduced. Some might argue that charitable giving would fall. Thus, charitable institutions might seek additional subsidies, either through the tax system or through federal government outlays, if the income tax is restructured.

So all these itemized deductions might be trimmed back in particular details. An alternative approach would be a more general cutback of all itemized deductions. The Kennedy administration proposed a ''floor'' on itemized deductions, so that only total deductions in excess of some fraction of adjusted gross income (in the Kennedy proposal, 5 percent) would be deductible.[13] Another approach suggested at the end of the Johnson administration was to allocate deductions between taxable and nontaxable income, so that the fraction of deductible expenses that was implicitly paid for from income not taxed (because of personal exemptions, for example) would not be deductible.[14]

Yet another approach would limit deductions by in effect converting them to credits (as was discussed in the context of the mortgage interest deduction). This approach responds to the ''upside-down subsidy'' problem, whereby high-income taxpayers save more from an additional dollar of deductions (under the current law, a maximum of 50 percent) than do lower-income taxpayers (a minimum of 11 percent, or zero if the person is not taxable or does not itemize). This problem applies to all itemized deductions; the federal government implicitly pays more of the state and local taxes of a wealthy taxpayer, and makes larger implicit matching grants to the charities supported by wealthy persons, for example. To deal with this problem, one current tax proposal limits deductions to apply to the lowest (14 percent) tax

12. ''Unpolished Strategem,'' *Wall Street Journal*, June 8, 1983, p. 1.

13. Congressional Quarterly, *Congress and the Nation* (Washington, D.C.: Congressional Quarterly, 1965), pp. 434–36.

14. Committee on Ways and Means, U.S. House of Representatives, and Committee on Finance, U.S. Senate, *Tax Reform Studies and Proposals: U.S. Treasury Department*, February 5, 1969, part 2, pp. 148–52.

rate, which is the rate at which about 70 percent of all taxpayers would pay tax.[15] For the top 30 percent of taxpayers who would pay at higher rates, an additional dollar of deductions would decrease taxes by the same fourteen cents. Another proposal explicitly converts the deductions into credits, with the credit rate varying from item to item.[16]

A final approach is to reduce all deductions proportionately, say, by 10 percent.[17] Although the major function of such a proposal is to raise revenue, it would also make the tax system more neutral (to the extent that itemized deductions are incentives, rather than compensation for hardship or costs of earning income). This approach can also be generalized to include tax credits and business subsidies, thereby enhancing its revenue gain and perhaps its political appeal. The major difficulty is complexity. The reduction of itemized deductions would add to the computational load of the taxpayer. Furthermore, pressure would certainly build over time to exclude certain deductions, such as employee business expenses (which should be allowed in full to define net income) or charitable contributions (which might be exempted for their inducement to philanthropy). Any such exceptions would substantially increase the complexity of this approach. If taxpayers came to anticipate the granting of such exceptions at some future date, they would alter their behavior in undesirable ways (such as postponing charitable giving).

Employee Benefits. Employers may deduct their costs of employee compensation in computing their taxable income. These costs include not only wages in cash but also fringe benefits including life, health, and dental insurance premiums, on-site day care, and contributions to pension plans (with the last of these subject to a generous maximum amount). Logic suggests that these benefits are income to employees and so should be taxable to them. Employees are required to pay tax only on their cash compensation, however, and so neither the employer nor the employee pays tax on fringe benefits. The rationale for this subsidy is to encourage the provision of these benefits. The tax exclusions for employer-provided insurance and day care will cost about $23 billion in revenue in fiscal 1985, and the exclusion for pension contributions will cost about $54 billion.[18] These provisions are among the fastest growing tax expenditures in terms of revenue loss. Defenders of the exclusions argue that without a tax preference, the federal government would

---

15. The Bradley-Gephardt Fair Tax Act.

16. The Hatfield Simpliform Tax Act. For example, taxpayers receive a 20 percent credit for charitable contributions but a 15 percent credit for home mortgage interest.

17. This proposal was made by Rep. Pete Stark.

18. Joint Committee on Taxation, *Estimates of Federal Tax Expenditures*, table 1, pp. 9–16.

be forced to provide these benefits directly and that providing such benefits as national health insurance would cost more than subsidizing private insurance through the tax system.

Realistically, though, employees would not abandon private life and health insurance if the tax subsidy were repealed, because such insurance coverage is really a necessity and the private mode is the most efficient way to provide it. Employers would not drop such coverage for their employees because group plans are the most economical approach, and employees would bargain for the coverage. Thus, it seems unlikely that repeal of the tax exemption would lead to government provision of life and health insurance for workers (beyond the aspects of such insurance already provided through Social Security). Some other employer-paid benefits might change without a tax exemption, however. Dental insurance, for example, is a much less common form of compensation, and probably much less necessary. The federal government surely would not feel compelled to provide dental insurance for employees if the tax exclusion were repealed. Where employers have provided on-site day care, the reasons probably are the convenience and flexibility the day care affords to employees. Given their advantages, such programs should not need a tax preference to survive. Employer-provided pensions add a useful incentive to save for retirement. The major structural problem is that pension programs can be manipulated by highly compensated employees to provide substantial tax savings, probably well in excess of what would be necessary to encourage prudent provision for retirement.

The tax exemption for fringe benefits distorts employee choices. Because fringe benefits are cheaper than other goods and services (after the tax exemption is taken into account), employees want more of them. The more they get, the narrower the tax base becomes and the higher tax rates must be, implicitly, to meet the government's revenue needs. The higher the tax rates, the greater the incentive to ask for compensation in the form of fringe benefits, and so the vicious circle continues. Considerable effort is now expended in maximizing tax-exempt compensation, including the so-called cafeteria plans.[19]

Very little can be accomplished in tax restructuring without touching the employee benefit exclusion, simply because its revenue cost is so large and fast-growing. Recent attempts by both the administration and the Congress to cut back the revenue loss have proved futile; in particular, the administra-

---

19. Cafeteria plans give employees a budget that they may allocate among different forms of tax-exempt compensation however they wish. Timothy B. Clark, "On the Fringe—1985 Could Be the Year Congress Zeroes in on Employee Benefits," *National Journal*, July 14, 1984, pp. 1356–61.

tion's proposal for a relatively ambitious cap on tax-free health insurance premiums (limiting tax-exempt contributions to $175 per month for families and $70 per month for individuals) has gone nowhere. Broad-based restructuring with lower marginal rates as partial compensation could stand a better chance. A long step toward a broadened tax base would be to repeal the exclusion for insurance premiums and day care and to reduce the limit on tax-free contributions to pension funds.

Saving and Investment Incentives. As was noted in the preceding chapter, many experts argue that our economy suffers from insufficient saving and investment. Some believe that the fault lies with our tax system and that greater tax incentives are needed. Recent legislation has provided many such incentives. Prominent among them are the Individual Retirement Account (IRA) and Keogh tax-favored retirement saving provisions, the exclusion for long-term capital gains, the investment tax credit (ITC), and the Accelerated Cost Recovery System (ACRS) for investment in depreciable business assets. IRAs and Keoghs will cost $11 billion in lost revenues in fiscal 1985, the ITC about $35 billion, and ACRS about $23 billion.[20]

As was argued earlier, however, there is little evidence that total saving is sensitive to tax policy. For example, the expanded IRA provisions were labeled a resounding success in terms of participation, with 11.4 million taxpayers using them in 1982;[21] but the personal saving rate declined in that year.[22] Part of the problem is that taxpayers can reduce their taxes through IRAs without actually saving by moving money from a standard bank account to an IRA. Similarly, the ITC, ACRS, and the exclusion for long-term capital gains can be combined with other tax preferences and creative financing to build tax shelters that reduce taxes without increasing productive investment. Furthermore, because these provisions reduce total tax revenue, they force statutory tax rates up. That means that all saving (and work effort) in forms that are not tax-preferred is discouraged. Given the manipulation that these provisions encourage and the necessarily higher statutory rates they require, the economy may be worse off for having these large tax incentives for saving and investment.

The 60 percent exclusion for long-term capital gains is intended to encourage risky investments and to compensate for inflation. As was discussed

---

20. Joint Committee on Taxation, *Estimates of Federal Tax Expenditures*, table 1, pp. 9–16. The ACRS tax expenditure is measured relative to straightline depreciation for structures and accelerated depreciation for equipment over the full tax lives used in the pre-1981 tax system.

21. Dorothea Riley, "Individual Income Tax Returns: Selected Characteristics from the 1982 Taxpayer Usage Study," *Statistics of Income Bulletin*, vol. 3, Summer 1983, p. 43.

22. *Economic Report of the President*, February 1984, table B-23, p. 248.

in the preceding chapter, the exclusion is a most inexact compensation for inflation; and it is of questionable help in encouraging investment, though there is some evidence that it steers some investment toward new ventures. The exclusion significantly complicates the tax system and is an important element in many tax shelter arrangements. If the capital gains exclusion could be repealed, it would permit a substantial reduction of the marginal tax rates in the highest brackets, where a disproportionate share of the capital gains income would be taxed.

Some experts argue for indexing the cost basis of capital gains to remove the portion caused by inflation.[23] As was noted in the preceding chapter, indexing only an income item without indexing debt would allow manipulation and tax avoidance. Indexing only capital gains income would allow taxpayers to borrow and deduct their nominal interest, invest the proceeds, and pay tax only on their real capital gains. This is the same kind of arbitrage in which taxpayers now engage to take advantage of the capital gains exclusion.

The mere reduction of tax rates is itself an incentive to saving and investment. The point of the incentives now in the law is to reduce the tax on particular forms of saving and investment, in some cases all the way to zero. Income tax restructuring would reduce the rates on *all* forms of saving and investment, though not to zero, and would do this with less distortion. Full tax exemptions of only selected investments can encourage manipulation and abuse, as in the tax shelters encouraged by ACRS.

In sum, saving and investment incentives have a less-than-inspiring track record, and their use in tax shelters has been an embarrassment to the tax system in general. Lower tax rates across-the-board could well be better for the tax system and the economy.

Oil and Gas Preferences. The two major subsidies for the oil and gas industry—the expensing of intangible drilling costs and percentage depletion—have a revenue cost in fiscal 1985 of about $4 billion.[24] Oil and gas firms can expense their intangible costs (labor and supplies) of drilling productive wells, whereas other businesses would have to capitalize such costs and deduct them over the productive life of a project. Percentage depletion allows small, nonintegrated oil firms (not the major firms that own their own refineries and distribution networks) to deduct a percentage of the cost of oil-

---

23. Roger E. Brinner, "Inflation and the Definition of Taxable Personal Income," in Henry J. Aaron, ed., *Inflation and the Income Tax* (Washington, D.C.: The Brookings Institution, 1976), pp. 121–45.

24. Joint Committee on Taxation, *Estimates of Federal Tax Expenditures*, table 1, pp. 9–16.

producing land each year. Over the life of a well these deductions can exceed the investment in the well several times over.

Both these preferences were intended to encourage the domestic oil industry, but market conditions have changed dramatically in recent years. In the 1950s and 1960s, the rationale for the preferences was to protect the domestic industry against cheap oil from the Middle East. Then in the 1970s, when the world oil price soared, the rationale was to increase domestic supply. Now, when worldwide conservation and slow economic growth have decreased demand, these preferences are sometimes defended as support for an ailing industry.

The dominant factors in today's domestic oil market are geology and demand, not the tax law. Some domestic firms are hurting not because they are earning income and it is being taxed away, but because they are not earning income in the first place. Taxing the oil industry on the same terms as other industries are taxed will encourage a more rational allocation of resources in the economy. The high world market price for oil, well in excess of many producing nations' costs of production, will provide more than adequate incentives to explore for and develop new sources of oil.

A Critical Mass. Clearly, all taxpayers can look at the list of tax preferences and reach their own conclusions about which are justified and which are not. Scientific judgment cannot determine what social, political, or even economic purposes are so important that the federal government must intervene in the market process through tax subsidies. Every judgment on the tax base is to some degree subjective.

But some objective factors cannot be ignored. The Congress followed a base-broadening strategy in 1982 and again in 1984, but it raised too little revenue to tame the deficit, much less to allow additional cuts in tax rates. Further small-scale efforts seem prohibitively painful. If the deficit is to be reduced and tax rates are to be cut as well to ease the pain, the big preferences enumerated here must be part of the plan. Without some action on the big items, there simply is not enough revenue to be gained on other provisions. But with a much broadened base, the revenue gained from repealing any one additional provision would pay for a tax rate cut to mollify the losers of all other repealed preferences. A "critical mass" of base broadening is necessary to make the entire package attractive.

There is thus a kind of political "chicken and egg" problem: if rates remain relatively high, taxpayers will not part with their preferences; but if preferences are not repealed, tax rates cannot be cut. The political difficulty caused by this dilemma is discussed later.

Low-Income Relief

Chapter 2 noted that inflation has substantially eroded the personal exemptions and zero-bracket amounts since they were last increased in 1978. For this reason, the tax burden on low-income households has increased sharply.

The personal exemptions and zero-bracket amounts are referred to as "low-income relief" because they eliminate entirely the tax burden for households with very low incomes. Of course, these provisions cut taxes for persons with higher incomes as well, although many middle-income and most upper-income households itemize their deductions and therefore receive no direct benefit from the zero-bracket amount.

As was explained in chapter 2, the 1981 tax cuts ignored the effect of inflation on low-income taxpayers through the erosion of the exemptions and the zero-bracket amount. Instead, it gave generous tax rate cuts to middle- and upper-income persons—cuts that more than offset inflation; the tax rate cuts for low-income persons did not fully offset the erosion of the exemption and zero-bracket amount. Low-income persons had to wait until 1985 for indexation of the exemption and the zero-bracket amount for subsequent inflation; but the indexing provision in the law corrects only for inflation occurring during and after 1984. There is still no compensation for the inflation from 1978 through 1983, when the damage was done. Any tax restructuring must in fairness redress this mistreatment of low-income taxpayers; the only question is how.

One recent proposal is to double the personal exemption (from $1,000 to $2,000).[25] This approach would remedy the problem of low-income taxpayers, but it would cause other problems. A doubled exemption would cause a minimum loss in revenue of $30 billion in 1985 under the current law.[26] Under a graduated rate system, much of that tax relief would go not to lower-bracket but to upper-bracket taxpayers, especially those with large families (who could claim more exemptions). But upper-income taxpayers received generous tax cuts in 1981. Furthermore, large revenue losses at the upper end of the scale through a bigger exemption would preclude some reduction in the marginal tax rate for those taxpayers, and it is rate reduction that increases economic efficiency.

---

25. The Kemp-Kasten Fair and Simple Tax (FAST) Act of 1984 and the Treasury Department's proposal of November 1984.

26. Assuming 200 million exemptions were claimed at an average effective tax rate of 15 percent.

It would make more sense to put greater emphasis on increasing the zero-bracket amount. A higher zero-bracket amount gives the same tax relief that a higher exemption does to low-income households, but most upper-income taxpayers would not benefit because they itemize their deductions. Thus, for any given target level of tax burden for upper-income persons, marginal tax rates can be slightly lower with a larger zero-bracket amount than with a larger exemption. Furthermore, a larger zero-bracket amount can be a significant simplication for some middle-income taxpayers who would claim the zero-bracket amount rather than itemizing; for them, the bother of computing and recording all their itemized deductions would be eliminated.

Another part of low-income relief in the current tax law is the earned-income credit for low-income families with children. Under this credit, families with income from labor receive a credit equal to 11 percent of their wage income, with a maximum $550 credit, phased down to zero at $11,000 of income. If the credit exceeds the tax otherwise due, the excess is refundable to the family in cash.

The earned-income credit is a far-from-perfect policy instrument, as was pointed out earlier. It is exceedingly complicated; many low-wage workers who have no tax withheld and are not legally required to file may inadvertently miss out on the credit; and unless the employer does some complicated paperwork, the employee receives the credit as a lump sum after the end of the tax year, making it an awkward income support policy. Nonetheless, no other tax provision helps low-wage workers with children and offsets the burden of the Social Security payroll tax. The credit was substantially eroded from 1978 until 1984 (when it was increased from 10 percent, with a maximum of $500), and it could be increased further despite its practical shortcomings.

Tax Rates

A major objective of restructuring the income tax is lower marginal tax rates. Cuts in the tax rates are the payoff of tax restructuring, and as such would be highly visible and controversial.

There are two aspects of tax rate reduction: how much rates can be cut on average over all taxpayers, and how much rates would change at different income levels. The potential overall reduction in tax rates would be determined by the revenue needed to control the deficit and the degree of base broadening attained. In a sense, repealing any tax preference would "buy" a tax rate cut. The job is to find every tax preference that is less beneficial than its alternative tax rate cut. As was noted earlier, enough base broadening can achieve a "critical mass," allowing tax rates sufficiently low that repeal of the preferences is tolerable. But repeal of just a few preferences may allow only small rate cuts, to many people not worth the bother.

How much tax rates could be cut at different income levels (from the range under the current law of 11 percent to 50 percent) depends on two more factors: what the target distribution of the tax burden is, and what income groups are most affected by the tax base broadening. For purposes of discussion, a possible tax bill could be split into two parts: restructuring (which would broaden the tax base and reduce the tax rates but leave total revenue unchanged) and deficit reduction (which would increase the restructured tax rates to raise the needed additional revenue). One conclusion of chapter 2 was that any redistribution of the tax burden in a restructured income tax would be contentious. One way around that minefield in restructuring would be not to change the tax distribution at all (apart from offsetting the effects of recent inflation on low-income taxpayers). Keeping the tax load of each income group constant minimizes the trauma in the changeover to a new system. In contrast, shifting the tax load from one group to another imposes unnecessary pain on the losers, and so should be avoided. Thus, our rare tax increases have either spread the necessary pain as thinly as possible (the Vietnam War surtax) or targeted on specific areas of abuse or excessive generosity (the 1982 and 1984 tax bills). And considering that tax revenues ultimately must be increased, we must take care not to overload any particular income group.

This makes the so-called flat-rate tax a nonstarter. Table 10 shows that the current tax system is generally progressive, despite the existing tax preferences. Imposing a constant-revenue flat tax would reduce the burden on the highest-income groups. The large personal exemptions needed to protect the poor and near-poor would place a heavier burden on the middle-income groups. The problem is very simple: Because the highest income groups pay about 25 percent of their total income in tax, no flat tax at any lower rate can exact the current level of liabilities from them. Someone will have to pick up the slack, and with large exemptions for the low-income groups, middle-income taxpayers are the only ones left. If the tax rate were then increased to reduce the deficit, the burden on the middle-income groups would increase even more. Most people probably would call this unfair.

Some people argue that the flat tax is the only fair tax, because only under a single tax rate does everyone pay at the same rate. This logic has problems. Everyone pays at the same rate only if there is no exemption or deduction of any kind, and if that is true, then the poorest of the poor must pay income tax. The fairness of such a tax would be questionable. But if exemptions and deductions are allowed, then the tax rate must change to raise any given amount of revenue. An infinite variety of combinations of rates

TABLE 10

EFFECTS OF ALTERNATIVE "FLAT-RATE" TAX SYSTEMS

Expanded Income Class[a]	Tax as a Percentage of Adjusted Gross Income, 1984 Law	Percentage Change in Tax	
		Pure Flat Tax[b]	Flat Tax with Low-Income Relief[c]
Under $5,000	0.9	1,259.6	395.3
5,000–10,000	4.8	147.4	−7.4
10,000–15,000	7.5	57.3	1.4
15,000–20,000	9.2	28.8	7.7
20,000–30,000	10.5	12.8	9.3
30,000–50,000	12.4	−5.1	7.8
50,000–100,000	16.7	−29.2	−6.7
100,000–200,000	22.3	−47.1	−23.1
200,000 and over	25.2	−53.2	−27.7
Average	11.8	−0.3	0.1

SOURCE: Joint Committee on Taxation.

a. Expanded income is adjusted gross income plus tax preferences included in the base of the minimum tax, less investment interest expense to the extent of investment income.

b. An 11.8 percent tax on adjusted gross income plus the excluded portion of long-term capital gains.

c. An 18.7 percent tax on adjusted gross income plus the excluded portion of long-term capital gains, less a $1,500 per person exemption and $3,000 ($6,000 for married couples) standard deduction (no itemized deductions allowed).

and exemptions can be imagined; the choice is necessarily subjective. And if subjective judgment is required, there is no reason why the range of alternatives should be restricted to single-rate taxes. The best tax rate structure will be the one that the people collectively choose through a surely contentious political process, and that choice must be a graduated rate structure if the current distribution of the tax burden is to be continued.

Holding the tax burden constant in a restructured tax does not necessarily mean a simple across-the-board reduction of tax rates, either in absolute or in percentage terms. In fact, the shape of the rate schedule might change significantly. If capital gains were taxed in full and if itemized deductions were cut back or capped in some way, the taxable incomes of upper-income groups would increase substantially. As a result, their tax rates could be cut more than the average in percentage terms at no loss of revenue. And if personal exemptions and zero brackets were increased to catch up with post-1978 inflation, the lowest tax rate might even be increased slightly. The tax load of the poor and near-poor would still be reduced, because the exemption and standard deduction have a much stronger effect than the bottom-bracket tax rate in determining the liabilities of low- and moderate-income taxpayers.

The lowest tax rates are not an important incentive or an efficiency issue, because their level is so low that they do not impinge on incentives to any real extent; a tax of 10 to 15 percent surely does not significantly decrease work incentives or distort economic choices. So the tax rate schedule might be significantly flatter, higher at the bottom and lower at the top, without changing the distribution of the tax burden. Several congressional proposals follow this pattern.

After the tax system is restructured to maintain current revenues, the deficit remains as a crucial issue. With a broad tax base, raising tax rates could be an acceptable remedy. In fact, if the tax base is significantly broadened, the tax rates become so powerful that only a few percentage points would suffice to yield the likely revenue target (for example, a 10 percent surtax on a 30 percent maximum rate would add only three percentage points). How the additional burden should be apportioned—whether rates should be increased across the board or only for upper-income groups—is a matter of personal judgment. The data reported in chapter 2 do suggest, however, that upper-income taxpayers received the greatest relief from the 1981 tax cuts.

The only remaining issue concerning tax rates is whether the boundaries of the rate brackets should be indexed for inflation, as the 1981 law provided (starting in 1985). Indexing can be defended as almost a moral issue; taxes should be determined by real rather than nominal income. According to this point of view, the "bracket creep" that occurs without indexation can be seen as a secret and underhanded way for the federal government to increase taxes and expand its spending. And the reduced revenue growth with indexing unquestionably forces the government to face up to tough spending choices.

Figure 8, however, shows that the federal government has not used bracket creep to continually expand its spending. Income tax liabilities spiked upward in wartime, and grew rapidly through the inflation of 1978 to 1981, but always returned to approximately 10.5 percent of personal income. The Congress and the president have felt compelled to return any revenue from bracket creep to the taxpayers (although chapter 2 showed that this relief has been distributed in different patterns at different times). In 1981, virtually all observers agree, there would have been a tax cut regardless of who occupied the White House. And although bracket creep may have been a secret a decade ago, by now virtually everyone in the country is conscious of it. Without indexation, voters would hold their representatives accountable for keeping the income tax within bounds.

The unfortunate fact is that taxes must be increased to help to contain the budget deficit. Logically, we should explore every possible way to increase revenues, and allowing the exemptions and tax-rate brackets to remain unchanged through a year or more of mild inflation (such as the mid-1980s

FIGURE 8

FEDERAL INDIVIDUAL INCOME TAX LIABILITY AS A PERCENTAGE OF PERSONAL INCOME
1946–1983

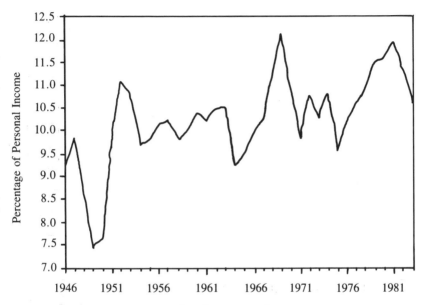

SOURCE: *The National Income and Product Accounts of the United States, 1929–1976 Statistical Tables; Economic Report of the President,* February 1984; and *Survey of Current Business,* June 1984.

level) is one option. Indexing the tax-rate brackets closes off that option. Indexing increases the need for painful discretionary tax increases, and thus may reduce the chances of success against the deficit. And if the economy should ever reenter a period of excess demand inflation, automatic indexing, by reducing money tax collections, will make that inflation somewhat harder to stop.

No one would advocate financing the federal government over the long haul through bracket creep, but the historical record does not suggest that this is a danger. Indexing the tax brackets and exemptions is not a complicated task, and its effects may not be large in a restructured income tax. But indexing would make the job of controlling the deficit that much harder. In the short term, repealing indexing, or limiting indexing in some way (either indexing only the personal exemption and zero brackets, or indexing only for the excess of inflation over 2 or 3 percent per year) should at least be considered as a defense against the deficit.

Congressional Tax Proposals

As has been noted earlier, several tax proposals along these general lines have been submitted to the Congress. There was a rush of interest in income tax alternatives in 1982, generating mostly a number of unrealistic flat-rate proposals. These proposals would have eliminated politically crucial tax deductions and would have reduced federal tax revenues or redistributed the tax burden from wealthy to middle- and low-income taxpayers, or both. Among these proposals, however, was the Bradley-Gephardt Fair Tax Act of 1982, which retained the most politically sensitive deductions and used graduated tax rates to maintain total federal revenues and the current distribution of the tax burden. This bill subsequently was modified as the Fair Tax Act of 1983 to conform to changes in the law made by the Tax Equity and Fiscal Responsibility Act of 1982. Two further pieces of legislation along these lines (revenue and distributional neutrality and continuation of important tax preferences) were the Hatfield Simpliform Tax Act and the Quayle SELF (an acronym for simplicity, efficiency, low rates, and fairness) Tax Act.

A fourth and later piece of legislation was the Kemp-Kasten FAST (an acronym for fair and simple tax) Tax Act, introduced in 1984. FAST used a flat-tax format rather than graduated rates, but retained some progressivity by excluding 20 percent of labor earnings up to the amount of the Social Security wage base (that is, the amount of wages or self-employment income subject to Social Security payroll tax—$39,600 in 1985). FAST has two serious problems. First, it causes the government to lose significant amounts of revenue (unless increases in economic activity are assumed), which is difficult to reconcile with the deficit problem. Second, its revenue loss is distributed solely as a tax cut for the highest-income taxpayers, while low- and middle-income taxpayers are held even or face a slight tax increase; hence, such a tax is bound to raise issues of fairness.[27]

Although the Bradley-Gephardt, Hatfield, and Quayle bills differ in detail,[28] their essential features are close enough to be considered together in the legislative process. Given an agreement on the basis of objectives of continuity in the income tax framework, including a relatively short list of deductions and maintenance of the amount and distribution of tax revenues,

---

27. Letter from David Brockway, chief of staff, Joint Committee on Taxation, to Sen. Robert Dole, chairman, Senate Finance Committee, August 6, 1984.

28. Among the differences, the Hatfield Simpliform Tax Act would convert itemized deductions to tax credits at varying rates, whereas the Bradley-Gephardt Fair Tax would cap deductions; and the Quayle SELF Tax Act in a revised version would convert business tax depreciation to immediate expensing, whereas the Bradley-Gephardt bill would use depreciation.

the remaining provisions of the tax law are easier to determine in a political context.

The greatest popular interest would probably rest on the distributional effects of the tax bills. Variation with individual circumstance would be unavoidable, but replicating the pattern of the current law by income group is a simple matter of adjustment of low-income relief provisions and tax-rate brackets. The distribution of the tax burden would be little changed among income groups, although within each income group virtually all taxpayers would face some slight shifting in one direction or the other.

In sum, these initiatives from the Congress would fulfill the goals of greater simplicity of tax filing and economic decisions, greater fairness in the distribution of the tax burden among taxpayers, and increased economic efficiency. In part because these proposals demonstrated the potential of tax reform, interest in the topic grew and other players came forward.

The Treasury Tax Proposals

In late November 1984, the Treasury Department responded to President Reagan's request in his State of the Union message of that year for a comprehensive study of tax simplification and reform.[29] Like the congressional proposals and this analysis, the Treasury rejected the options of the personal expenditure tax, the flat-rate income tax, and the value-added or national sales tax. The Treasury followed the general pattern of the congressional proposals enumerated above, using an income tax with graduated tax rates, but it differed in some significant ways.

Distribution of Revenues. First, the Treasury chose to maintain total federal income tax revenues, but to shift the tax burden somewhat from the individual to the corporate tax. Thus, individual income taxes would be cut, on average, by approximately 8.5 percent, while corporate taxes would be increased to make up the difference. Because revenues from the individual income tax are much larger than those from the corporate tax, the corporate increase in percentage terms must be substantially larger—about 25 to 30 percent.[30]

---

29. U.S. Department of the Treasury, *Tax Reform for Fairness, Simplicity, and Economic Growth: The Treasury Department Report to the President* (Washington, D.C.: U.S. Government Printing Office, November 1984), 2 vols.

30. As was noted earlier, the CBO 1989 revenue forecast calls for about $500 billion of individual tax revenues and about $100 billion from the corporate tax. These relative proportions would suggest than an 8.5 percent individual income tax cut would require a corporate tax increase of more than 40 percent. The corporate increase figure in the Treasury proposals is lower because it assumes higher baseline corporate tax revenues. This assumption depends on economic growth faster than the growth projected by the CBO, rapid investment growth, low interest rates, and low inflation. All these factors interact with the Treasury's proposed depreciation system, described in the text.

The decrease in the individual income tax is greatest in percentage terms for lower-income taxpayers, largely because of a doubling of the personal exemption to $2,000; but all income groups receive a tax cut. The reductions range in size from almost one-third for taxpayers with incomes under $10,000, to 6.4 percent for taxpayers with $100,000 to $200,000 of income. (Taxpayers with incomes larger than $200,000 receive an 8.0 percent tax cut.) This reduction is achieved through a three-bracket tax-rate schedule, with rates of 15 percent, 25 percent, and 35 percent. A rough estimate of the reduction of tax burdens is shown in figure 9. Tax liabilities under the Treasury's proposal are lower than those under the Bradley-Gephardt proposal, which maintains the level of individual income tax revenues, and keeps their distribution virtually identical to that under the current law.

FIGURE 9

TAX BURDENS UNDER CURRENT LAW AND TWO RESTRUCTURING PROPOSALS

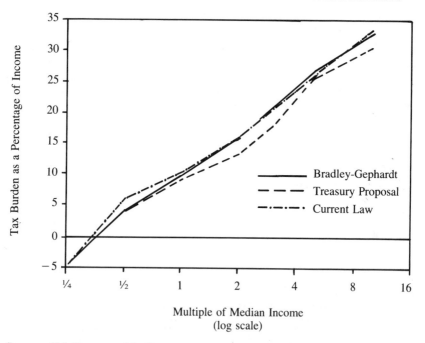

Multiple of Median Income
(log scale)

SOURCE: U.S. Departent of the Treasury, *Tax Reform for Fairness, Simplicity, and Economic Growth: The Treasury Department Report to the President* (Washington, D.C.: U.S. Government Printing Office, November 1984), vol. 1, p. xi, and computed by the author.

Indexation. A second important distinction between the proposal of the Treasury and those of the Congress is that the Treasury's would index the tax base for inflation. The undepreciated balance of the cost of depreciable business assets would be increased each year for inflation; with the removal of the effect of inflation, however, depreciation would mirror the actual loss of value of assets, with no acceleration. The cost basis of capital gains would be increased for inflation since 1965 (or the date of the purchase of the asset, whichever was later), but the adjusted basis would be taxed in full.

Both depreciation and capital gains indexation would involve some complexity, but indexation of interest income and expense would be far more complex, both in terms of the number of taxpayers and the number of transactions affected. To make this process more manageable, the Treasury proposes to adjust for inflation by rule of thumb rather than by precise indexation. Each year, the Treasury would publish a percentage figure for the amount of both interest expense and interest income that would be disregarded for inflation. The Treasury would derive that figure from the inflation rate and a general measure of interest rates. For example, if inflation were 4 percent and a representative interest rate were 10 percent, 40 percent of interest income would not be taxable, and 40 percent of interest expense would not be deductible. To ease the transition and provide relief for borrowers under long-term contracts, the Treasury proposal would exempt from indexation all home mortgage interest expense and an additional amount of interest expense equal to the taxpayer's interest income plus $5,000. In this form, the inflation adjustment would seldom be precise, and there is some danger that taxpayers with investment income could manipulate the form of their receipts to take advantage.[31] In addition, this inflation adjustment would add complexity, though it is simpler than precise indexation. Finally, because some interest expense is not indexed, the provision would lose revenue, and the exemption of mortgage interest expense could leave homeownership more tax favored than it is under the current law.

Dividend Relief. Another significant feature of the Treasury proposals is a deduction for corporations equal to half of the dividends they pay out. As was explained in the preceding chapter, dividend relief proposals such as this offset the double taxation of dividends in the existing law, which encourages firms to retain earnings rather than pay out dividends. Unlike actual integration (in which all corporate income, whether retained or paid out, is taxed only to shareholders), however, dividend relief schemes like the Trea-

---

31. Taxpayers with interest expense may find it advantageous to have their investment income characterized as interest, so that it can shield their interest expense from indexation.

sury's still influence corporations' dividend payout decisions, one way or the other, to some degree. Thus, the deduction for dividends paid does not attain complete neutrality, and it does not fully eliminate the double tax on dividends (because the deduction equals only half of dividends paid). Furthermore, it does cost revenue.

The Carter administration's leaked dividend relief proposal of 1977 aroused substantial opposition among corporate managers. It included a tax credit for household shareholders to offset the tax implicitly paid by corporations on the dividends they distribute. This credit would make dividends relatively more attractive to shareowners, who would demand that more of corporate income be paid out; such demands would reduce corporate managers' financial flexibility. The Treasury approach, giving corporations a deduction instead of giving shareowners a credit, would be less visible to shareowners and would directly cut taxes for corporations. Thus, it would be less offensive to corporate managers, though less attractive to shareholders. In the final analysis, however, because each additional dollar of dividends would reduce corporate taxes, shareholders understandably could clamor for more dividends under the Treasury plan, just as they could under the Carter administration approach.

The Treasury's corporate deduction is probably simpler than the shareholder credit approach, because the deduction does not require any additional reporting of information from corporations to shareholders or any additional computations by shareholders. It also avoids any contentious legislative decisions about how much tax credit shareholders should receive if their corporations pay little or no tax because of foreign tax credits, temporary losses, or any tax preferences.

But the Treasury's corporate deduction would lose more revenue than would the shareholder credit. Many corporate shares are owned by tax-exempt organizations, such as pension funds or university endowments. It is at least feasible to deny shareholder credit to such tax-exempts, reducing the revenue cost of dividend relief. It is less likely that corporations would be denied their deductions merely because some of their shares were owned by tax-exempts.

So the Treasury's proposal would reduce the double tax on corporate dividends, but it would not completely remove the influence of the federal tax system from corporations' decisions whether to retain or distribute their earnings. It also would cause the government to lose revenue, which would have to be recouped by raising taxes elsewhere. The Treasury approach to dividend relief would improve on the 1977 Carter administration options in that it would be less offensive to corporate managers, and simpler; at the same time, it would be less attractive to shareowners and would lose more revenue.

Itemized Deductions. The Treasury's proposal uses no global cutback on itemized deductions but is more restrictive than the congressional proposals in two different areas. The Treasury would repeal all deductions for state and local taxes. This is an additional simplification, but it would put financial pressure on state and local governments if taxpayers lobbied for tax cuts (or opposed tax increases) because of the lack of federal deductibility.

The Treasury also recommended restricting the deduction for charitable contributions to those over 2 percent of income. In theory, this step eliminates the deductibility of small, routine contributions, but retains the incentive for making large contributions. In practice, it may be seen as removing the incentive for giving from moderate-income taxpayers who cannot afford large contributions. It also may be challenged as putting a roadblock in front of large contributions; because wealthy taxpayers would receive no tax savings from the deduction of the first 2 percent of their income, they might choose not to give at all. The 2 percent floor also might be circumvented to some degree if taxpayers were to "bunch" their deductions, making no contributions for several years and then making greater-than-normal contributions in one year. By so bunching their deductions, taxpayers would limit their non-deductible contributions to equal 2 percent of *one* year's income, rather than the sum of 2 percent of *every* year's income. Charitable institutions will probably be concerned by these prospects.

In sum, the Treasury's proposal achieves a greater degree of precision than the congressional bills, but it does so at the cost of greater complexity. Furthermore, the Treasury attains an attractive reduction in the tax burden on individuals, but it does so by raising the taxes of corporations. Many of the Treasury provisions could increase the political opposition to reform. It remains to be seen whether the Treasury's elaborations on the tax restructuring theme, as desirable as they are in theory, will justify their associated costs and make tax restructuring more likely.

Restructuring and the Deficit

The revenue yield of a restructured income tax obviously depends on both the tax base broadening that is done and the tax rates that are charged. The leading congressional proposals demonstrate that a restructured income tax could replace revenues under the current law with a maximum marginal tax rate no higher than 30 percent, while retaining some especially sensitive preferences (including the deductions for home mortgage interest and charitable contributions), and holding the distribution of the tax burden approximately constant.[32] The Treasury proposal has rates only slightly higher. To

---

32. The proposals fitting this description include the Bradley-Gephardt Fair Tax Act, the Hatfield Simpliform Tax Act, and the Quayle SELF Tax Act.

raise more revenue than the current law does, these proposals might have to
be toughened or supplemented by other taxes.

There is an important time dimension, however. Repeal or restriction of
tax preferences that are now growing faster than the economy, such as employer-paid fringe benefits, would yield increasing additional revenue in later
years even if revenue in the initial year were held equal to the current law.
So a restructured tax could start somewhat above current law revenues and
gradually make bigger inroads into the deficit.

Tax restructuring should not stop short of the necessary revenue yield,
however, by banking on supply-side "feedback" to provide the needed revenue. If the performance since 1981 is any indication, rate reductions are
unlikely to generate additional revenues in the late 1980s. Forecasts of new
revenues achieved through tapping the underground economy as well as earned
through faster growth of what is now legitimate economic activity must be
cautious. If the 1981 tax cuts did not provide such a revenue boost, there is
a great risk in pushing that strategy still further because deficits are already
dangerously large.

So the only prudent approach is to raise the necessary revenue with no
assumed change in taxpayer behavior. Tax rates can still be cut significantly,
even though total revenues are increased. If there is a revenue payoff to the
lower tax rates, those rates can always be cut further later.

We may not want to load all the deficit-reduction revenue burden onto
the income tax system. If not, there are some reasonable supplements. The
federal government has collected excise taxes on alcoholic beverages and
cigarettes for many years. These are specific excises, that is, calculated as
an amount of money per physical unit of product (per pack of cigarettes or
gallon of beverage). These taxes had been unchanged since 1954, and thus
considerably eroded by inflation, until the cigarette tax was increased in 1981
(and then partially reduced in 1984) and the tax on distilled liquor was increased in 1984. These excises could be increased further and still be lower
in real terms than they were in 1954. Doubling those taxes from their pre-
1981 level would raise about $6 billion per year by 1989.[33]

Another potential revenue raiser would be some form of excise tax on
energy. Some experts fear that the softness of the world oil price has made
consumers complacent about energy conservation, even though domestic proven
reserves appear to be on the decline. One response would be to impose an
energy tax (though one that would raise prices to less than their historical

---

33. Congressional Budget Office, *Reducing the Deficit: Spending and Revenue Options*
(Washington, D.C.: U.S. Government Printing Office, February 1984), pp. 237–39.

peak), thus encouraging conservation while reducing the deficit. Counterarguments are that an energy excise tax would increase prices and inflation, and would disproportionately hurt relatively energy-intensive industries and energy-dependent regions. An oil import fee of $4 per barrel (about 10 cents per gallon of product) would raise about $8 billion by fiscal 1989.[34]

Finally, in addition to broadening the base of the income tax, the federal government might try to increase revenues through greater enforcement of tax already due. The percentage of tax returns audited now is substantially below what it was in the 1970s: about 1.3 percent compared with 2.6 percent in 1976. Experience suggests that restoring audit coverage would increase revenues by almost $7 billion per year in excess of administrative costs.[35]

So the revenue burden on the income tax could be reduced somewhat to make the deficit-narrowing process more palatable. If we use $60 billion of total additional revenue in 1989 as a minimum goal, raising about $20 billion from other sources would reduce the additional load on the income tax to a minimum of $40 billion. That would require a surtax on a new tax law of less than 7 percent (on combined individual and corporate liabilities, assuming that the restructured law would just replace current law revenue before the surtax). Such a surtax would leave current congressional income tax proposals with maximum rates in the low 30 percent range, or lower if base broadening could be carried still further; the Treasury proposal would have a maximum individual tax rate of 37 or 38 percent.

So restructuring the income tax and narrowing the deficit gap is possible from the economic point of view. How about politics?

Politics—Can We Get There?

If tax returns could vote, a restructured income tax raising current revenues would win over today's tax law. The best evidence indicates that at least 60 percent of all tax returns would have a lower tax under a restructured law, even if it did not cut taxes overall and did not redistribute the tax burden.[36] The remaining tax returns would face tax increases, obviously larger on average than the tax cuts. Virtually all taxpayers, however, would face a lower marginal tax rate on extra income they earned, so the restructured tax would look like an even better deal.

---

34. Ibid., pp. 228–32.
35. Ibid., pp. 210–11.
36. Joseph J. Minarik, ''Yield of a Comprehensive Income Tax,'' in Joseph A. Pechman, ed., *Comprehensive Income Taxation* (Washington, D.C.: The Brookings Institution, 1977), pp. 277–98.

The popular advantage of a restructured tax is nothing new, however; American taxpayers could have had the same deal at any time for years. Why haven't they already insisted on it, and what are the implications for 1985 and beyond?

Experience teaches us these three key lessons about tax politics. First, not all taxpayers play the same role or carry the same weight in the political process. Second, what people think is true about tax policy may differ from reality, and what they want may exceed what they can have. And third, businesses as well as individuals play an important role in the legislative process. Each of these points has potentially important implications for tax policy.

Taxpayers and Voters

Contrary to the suggestion just made, tax returns do not vote; people do. And because voting and communication with members of Congress affect tax policy, we need to understand what difference this makes.

Different kinds of taxpayers participate in the political system to different degrees and in different ways. Probably the best available indicator of where individual taxpayers stand in the political system is their family status. Table 11, the latest (1982) IRS accounting of the types of taxpayers filing tax returns by their income level, shows that almost half of all single taxpayers have incomes under $10,000, while more than half of all married couples have incomes over $20,000. The low-income single taxpayers are generally young people. Some are students, still dependents of their parents, who file returns to reclaim withholding on their wages from summer and part-time jobs. Whether students or not, these relatively low-income single persons are probably less settled and more mobile, and thus have less influence in the political process, than people with higher incomes; or they are still a part of an older household and identify more with its interests. Thus, the number of tax returns filed in low-income groups probably overstates the impact of those groups on tax politics.

In contrast, the joint tax returns filed by couples represent people who are more settled geographically, and thus more likely to get a political hearing when they speak for their interests. Predictably, the joint returns in table 11 show significantly higher incomes on average than do the single returns. Thus, the political "center of gravity" is probably higher in income and social status than the level of the median tax return; the center of political influence is probably more like the median *joint* tax return.

TABLE 11

Amount and Sources of Income of Couples and Other Taxpayers, 1982

	Couples		Single and Other Taxpayers[a]	
Adjusted Gross Income Class	*Percentage of Joint Returns*	*Percentage of Income from Wages and Salaries*[b]	*Percentage of Other Returns*	*Percentage of Income from Wages and Salaries*[b]
Under 10,000	4.8	71.3	42.6	91.5
10,000–20,000	25.8	80.5	37.4	87.7
20,000–30,000	27.7	89.7	14.0	85.7
30,000–50,000	31.7	89.1	4.7	70.1
50,000–100,000	8.4	77.7	1.0	50.9
Over 100,000	1.6	54.8	0.2	28.5
TOTAL OR AVERAGE	100.0	84.4	100.0	82.6

Source: U.S. Department of the Treasury, Internal Revenue Service, *Statistics of Income— 1982 Individual Income Tax Returns*, table 3.2, pp. 77–79. Returns with negative incomes omitted.

a. Includes heads of households, married persons filing separate returns, and surviving spouses. Single returns constitute 80 percent of this group.

b. Author's estimates from 1981 IRS data.

The income level is important because a restructured tax system would affect different kinds of tax returns in different ways. The only unambiguous winners from income tax restructuring are people who receive all their income in forms that are taxable and who claim no itemized deductions; these people would have no change in the amount of their income subject to tax, and would benefit from lower tax rates and greater low-income relief. Most of these people probably live on modest amounts of wage income. As table 11 shows, it is at low-income levels that wages are the dominant form of income; above that level, other forms of income become relatively more important. Furthermore, as incomes grow into the middle range from joint returns, itemized deductions become more common; at still higher incomes, explicitly tax-motivated investments become attractive.

So income tax restructuring would be an unambiguous financial benefit only to the taxpayers who have the least political clout. For people who can get more of a hearing from the political process, restructuring the tax system would involve give-and-take—with tax rate cuts offsetting elimination of deductions and exclusions, and the net outcome in doubt. If these more politically involved people tend to vote their pocketbooks, it is not surprising that they would be hesitant about income tax restructuring.

Expectations and Reality

So people with median-range incomes and tax deductions have something to lose, as well as something to gain, from changes in the income tax. There are three layers of political resistance to be penetrated before the average voter will support tax reform.

First, public opinion polls reveal both dissatisfaction with the current income tax, and a lack of awareness of what would have to be done to fix it. Thus, the Harris poll of September 1982 showed that a bare plurality of the population believed that the traditional progressive income tax was "fair and equitable." A strong 62 percent favored a 14 percent flat-rate tax with no exemptions or deductions. But in the wake of that question, majorities or pluralities favored keeping seven key tax preferences that could not exist with the flat tax. Majorities could be found for repealing only oil and gas drilling cost deductions and political contributions tax credits.[37]

Thus, the public has an unrealistic notion of what tax restructuring can be. People want to make the tax more fair by repealing loopholes, but they fail to see provisions that they use as loopholes. Indeed, with tax returns private and with a complex tax code that few understand, people do not really know how they come out in the tax loophole "game." Even though statistics show that most taxpayers would pay lower taxes under a simpler law, the majority may not know or believe that. People who think that they can play the system better than the next taxpayer oppose simplification or reform. Until there is some realization that base broadening would have to touch just about everyone but that most taxpayers could still win on balance through the offsetting rate cuts, it is hard to imagine an informed consensus for tax reform.

A second layer of resistance goes beyond understanding what tax restructuring involves. Even if people realize and like what could be attained, they could still rationally resist any change. For voters with median-level incomes who have something to lose, tax restructuring is a risk. It involves opening up a tax code from which they receive some benefits and gambling those benefits in an uncertain legislative process. Although there is a quid pro quo implicit in the negotiations—"I'll give up my tax break if you cut my tax rates"—people are undoubtedly afraid that only half of the bargain will go through. And the tax bills of 1982 and 1984, which eliminated tax preferences but did not reduce tax rates, would reinforce that fear.

Thus, even though people dislike the current tax code, there is security in inaction. Taxpayers can take comfort in the deductions and exclusions they do claim and imagine that what would come out of the legislative process

---

37. "A Loss of Faith in the Progressive Tax," *Business Week*, September 6, 1982, p. 15.

(perhaps dominated by special interests) might be worse for them. The problem with tax reform from this point of view is that people cannot see the finished product until after they have paid for it.

A third layer of resistance to tax restructuring is the deficit. Opinions differ on how serious the deficit really is and whether it will continue. To people who belittle the importance of the deficit, even desirable tax restructuring could be a foot in the door for what they see as an unnecessary and harmful tax increase. The tax increase could more than wipe out any particular taxpayer's advantage from restructuring. This opinion, if widely held, would further erode support for a restructuring of the income tax.

But the deficit issue can cut both ways. If and when people understand the seriousness and persistence of the current deficits, tax reform could become more rather than less attractive. The taxpayer's first and understandable impulse is, "Don't raise my taxes." But if a tax increase is inevitable and the alternative is general tax increases based on the current tax system, the cry may change to, "Make sure that everyone else pays his share before you raise my taxes." On that kind of a playing field, tax restructuring stands a much better chance.

So the public's attitude toward the deficit problem could be crucial. The deficit could make people shun all discussion of taxes, even that aimed toward improvement and simplification of the law, fearing a double whammy of loss of deductions and a general tax increase. Or the deficit could convince people that a tax increase is unavoidable and lead them to demand that the increase be as fair as possible, even to the extent of redressing some long-standing problems.

On this last count, it is worth remembering some of the findings of chapter 2. The tax share of the deficit reduction effort in 1989 could be roughly equivalent to a 10 percent rate increase, as was discussed earlier in this chapter. Such an across-the-board rate increase would wipe out about half the 1981 rate cuts. Not only was the 1980 tax system the source of a political uprising, it also had the highest and most progressive tax burdens in recent history. Going halfway back toward 1980 is not an attractive option to many taxpayers. If this reality is understood—that painful tax increases will be necessary to reduce the deficit—then restructuring of the income tax could become a political prerequisite for action, not a roadblock.

Business and Tax Policy

It is not just households that influence tax policy; business and trade groups express their points of view as well. In part, businesses make their points through their employees and owners. Some people identify with their employers and express their employers' interests as their own, even though on tax policy their interests could be somewhat different. Corporate shareholders often feel the same.

Businesses can be very persuasive in pressing their interests. Businesses employ people; businesses are important parts of the communities where they are located and command a full hearing of their views. Owners of small businesses and executives of larger ones, again, are employers; as respected leaders of their communities, they belong to hospital boards and conduct charity drives. The interests of their businesses and the public interest tend to be identified with one another. Given this role, it is not surprising that businesses have considerable influence in the making of tax policy.

Unlike individuals, larger businesses deal with taxes twelve months a year. In part because of the complexity of the tax law and the opportunity to reduce tax liabilities, large corporations have permanent tax staffs for whom these issues are an occupation. Through these staffs, corporate executives are intensely aware of the tax law provisions that affect them. Associations of smaller businesses perform the same function for their members as the tax staffs of larger firms.

Because many businesses are taxed quite heavily at the margin (the highest corporate tax rate is 46 percent) and because some firms are so large, tremendous amounts of money can ride on individual provisions in the tax law. So just as corporations and trade associations can rationally hire permanent tax staffs, so they hire full-time lobbyists. People who lobby for businesses are paid to produce relative advantages for their clients.

Like individuals, businesses cannot foresee the final product of a piece of tax legislation, to express informed approval or disapproval from the beginning. Unlike individuals, however, businesses actively participate in the legislative process, expressing their interests on every provision of a bill throughout the debate. It is not in the nature of the business community to sign off on a complex piece of legislation that gives a little and takes a little, and leaves its net position approximately unchanged. Rather, it is in the interest of businesses, as it would be of any individual who was equally involved in the political process, to agree to any favorable provisions in a bill but to argue against any unfavorable ones, to try to get the best possible deal. In the current context, corporate representatives might expect that corporate tax rates would be cut in parallel to individual rates even if tax preferences important to corporations were not repealed. Thus, they might drive a hard bargain and hope to get the best of both worlds: lower tax rates and some continued preferences.

This attitude on the part of business groups is understandable and certainly not inappropriate. Most people see their personal efforts as promoting the national interest, and most people are right. In particular, the national interest is hardly consistent with a mass of business failures. But there are many important interests in the country, including the household sector (who are businesses' customers), and tax policy must *balance* those interests, not favor only one.

Another aspect of the role of business is the diversity of the business community. As the discussion of high-technology firms suggested, not all businesses have identical interests. In 1981, business marched essentially in lockstep for the Accelerated Cost Recovery System, even though high technology firms (among others) got little out of the deal. How different businesses would react to a tax increase that involved structural changes in the code is hard to predict.

Conclusion

It is simplistic to think of the passage of major tax legislation as a vote among the household population, or the business population, or even some weighted average of the two. Similarly, policy is not determined by an informed judgment on the long-run good of the country, because there is no agreement on just what that is. In the next few years, we might expect the short-run economic outlook to play an important role, with the indicators either spurring action through bad deficit news or suggesting a wait-and-see approach through good.

Whatever the precise role of public opinion and business interests, it is certain that they will have some influence. They are the most important factors that can be affected by the design of a tax package and the conduct of the legislative process. We might imagine circumstances that would maximize the chances for fundamental tax restructuring, even though nothing can guarantee action.

Implications

A thorough restructuring of the income tax would be one of the major legislative events of recent years. What would it take to achieve restructuring after the years of talk and campaign themes that have yielded so little? Although nothing and no one can guarantee a landmark piece of legislation, there are some apparent prerequisites for meaningful action.

The Deficit. For popular opinion to favor tax restructuring in reality as well as in the abstract, it is probably essential that the public see the true danger of the budget deficit. Many taxpayers see any tax bill, even a restructuring of the income tax without raising further revenue, as a potential pain in the pocketbook. So long as the large budget deficits are thought either benign or disappearing through natural forces, people might just as soon not take a chance. But if the magnitude of the deficits becomes better understood—if it becomes clearer that likely economic growth cannot eliminate the deficits—people could come to accept tax action as necessary. Once that reality is clear, people who feel victimized by the current tax system could reject more of the same as an option, in favor of fundamental reform. People who feel that others pay less than their fair share may choose to see fair shares assessed all around before all taxes are increased.

A **"Leading Runner."** One of the problems with past discussions of tax restructuring is that they were often abstract. This has caused at least two problems. Many people have unrealistic ideas of what can be achieved; these ideas are fed by proposals of low-rate flat taxes that would leave the federal deficit substantially larger, rather than smaller. If people come to believe in simplistic approaches, they will be disillusioned and angry when reality sets in. At the other extreme, some people have been left fearing the worst, thinking that any approach would leave them hopelessly worse off. These people may believe that losing any deduction or exemption would cost them money, without realizing that tax rate cuts as part of the deal could more than compensate and leave them better off. Many people may mistakenly think that they are winners under the current system, when in reality they are losers.

Both these extreme views might be moderated if people are made aware of one or more proposals that (1) meet our revenue needs (at least by achieving revenue neutrality) and (2) distribute the tax burden closely enough to the current law's pattern to avoid imposing serious hardship. If people understand the tax rates that are necessary to avoid swelling the already large deficits, they may begin to appreciate the limitations on tax policy. If they also see that those rates, although not microscopic, are at least significantly smaller than those under current law, they may understand the potential of restructuring. And both sides could see the trade-offs between tax preferences and tax rates that are at the heart of our policy choices for 1985. Thus, an identifiable, sound proposal could both dispel unrealistic expectations and show the true potential of tax reform.

A "leading runner" could provide a magnet for support from the majority of individual taxpayers who would gain, though often modestly, through tax restructuring. This could overcome the usual policy paralysis when a majority with little to gain is apathetic, handing control to a minority each of whose members has a lot to lose. Unless the majority interest is expressed, the chances of tax restructuring, or even deficit reduction, could be slim.

Finally, a sound tax reform proposal could be the only workable baseline for congressional deliberations. The alternative approaches usually considered are (1) to start with the current law and to rip out tax preferences wholesale or (2) to wipe the slate clean and start from scratch. Either approach might work as an individual's course of action, but both would cause serious problems for a committee. Starting from the current law would quickly begin the same item-by-item trench warfare that made the 1982 and 1984 laws so painful; each group would see itself singled out as its tax preference was brought to the firing line. Yet starting with a blank sheet of paper could quickly begin a bidding war, as the unassailable tax preferences were introduced into the law, and other interests tried to slip theirs in as well.

In contrast, starting with a package that meets the overall revenue and distribution targets imposes a discipline. Adding any tax preference obviously and immediately loses revenue, and requires higher tax rates or repealing some other preference or preferences. This enforces balanced change to an already satisfactory package. By starting on target and allowing only compensating adjustments, the range of the debate is limited to constructive areas.

Obviously, any baseline choice of tax preferences to repeal and tax rates to impose—including the Treasury's November 1984 recommendation and congressional proposals—will be subjective. But any choice of a tax system is subjective: there is no single correct tax system. The process might as well start with a subjective choice that meets the basic standards, rather than with an abstraction—or the current law—that no one wants.

Business. As was noted earlier in this chapter, businesses tend to be more "plugged in" to the tax legislative process than individuals are; corporations and trade associations have lobbyists who follow the issues full time. As a result, businesses lobby for their interests on every provision in the code, just as individuals with the same involvement and resources would do. Because tax restructuring is a delicate give-and-take over many tax provisions—ideally with no one winning or losing very much—allowing some taxpayers to get their way on every issue would quickly doom the entire effort. So although the process must recognize the legitimacy of business interests, just as it does all others, the process must force businesses, like individuals, to make a package deal. The target should be a deal in which business is neither a winner nor a loser in simple revenue terms, but one in which favorable and unfavorable changes pretty much balance out. In the longer run, with lower tax rates and a more uniform tax base, businesses, like individuals, should be better off as a group.

The Bottom Line

On the basis of recent history, the odds against fundamental tax restructuring seem impossibly long. But judging from popular opinion on the income tax and the need for revenue action on the budget, there may be a chance. The failings of years of tax policy—leaving us with a law short on compliance and respect—and of budget policy—leaving us short on cash—may lead the people and the Congress to take a step they have long feared and avoided.

To complete the analogy begun at the outset, the tax system is like a building in need of maintenance and repair. Postponing the repair has imperceptible effects from year to year, but potentially disastrous long-run consequences. Repair is costly, and if done improperly can cause damage of its own. When structural deterioration begins, delaying repair becomes increasingly risky. Eventually, the building might need to be torn down and replaced.

The choice rests on our assessment of the state of the income tax. People will differ on the extent of needed repair, and the urgency; but given recent trends in the economy and in the tax system, repair cannot be postponed indefinitely.